A N D
QUEENS
OF BRITAIN

David Lambert and Randal Gray

HarperCollins*Publishers*

HarperCollins Publishers
P.O. Box, Glasgow G4 0NB

A Diagram Book first created by Diagram Visual
Information Limited of 195 Kentish Town Road,
London NW5 8SY, England

First published 1991
© Diagram Visual Information Limited 1991
Reprint 10 9 8 7 6 5 4 3 2 1 0

ISBN 0 00 458954 8

Coats of arms drawn by Kyri Kyriacou
Dynastic charts designed by Dino Skeete
Picture research by Patricia Robertson

Picture source acknowledgements
British Library (MSS. Cotton Caligula A VIII,
Tiberius A III, Claudius VI, Nero D VI; MS. Stowe
944; MS. Add 33241; MS. Roy 20 A II; MSS. Jul
EIV; MS. Harley 4632); Burgerbibliothek, Berne
(MS. Cod. 120); Corpus Christi College,
Cambridge (MS. 16); Corpus Christi College,
Oxford (MS. CCC 157); The Duke of Buccleuch
and Queensbury (Writhe's Garter Book); The
Duke of Roxburghe (Kelso Abbey Charter); The
Governing Body of Christ Church, Oxford (MS.
Walter de Millemetc); National Portrait Gallery
(George II by Townshend); Public Record Office E
368/69 (Edward I), KB 27/819 (Edward IV) and
MPF 366 (Darnley)

Printed in Great Britain by
HarperCollins Manufacturing, Glasgow

Introduction

The Collins *Gem Guide to Kings and Queens of Britain* is an absorbing and highly informative guide to a major theme in British history, listing British monarchs in a chronological sequence in which pre-1066 Norman Conquest rulers are grouped by tribe, region or country, and subsequent crowned heads by dynastic house. Dynastic charts clarify the family trees of the nine English (since 1066) and three Scottish (843-1567) royal houses, and introduce the relevant dynasty. The book also contains much valuable information that is not easily accessible elsewhere, for example, on the Scandinavian rulers of England, and on Welsh and Irish princes and kings.

Each sovereign's name appears in **bold** type, and every English king and queen since Athelstan (924-939) has a list of personal data followed by a brief summary of his or her reign. Wherever possible, contemporary imagery has been used to illustrate the monarch's life.

The Collins *Gem Guide to the Kings and Queens of Britain* offers an unrivalled wealth of concise, easy-to-consult information on British rulers, and is an invaluable companion for students of history at all levels, writers, researchers and journalists, or indeed for anyone with an interest in the history of these islands.

Contents

1 **ANCIENT BRITISH KINGS AND QUEENS** 6

2 **ROMAN AND ROMANO-BRITISH RULERS** 9

3 **ANGLO-SAXON MONARCHIES** 13
   Kings of Kent 15
   Kings of Sussex 18
   Kings of Essex 20
   Kings of East Anglia 22
   Kings of Mercia 25
   Kings of Northumbria 30
   Kings of Wessex 36
   Kings of England 43
   Scandinavian Kings in Britain 56

4 **WELSH KINGS AND PRINCES** 66

5 **IRISH KINGS** 76

6 **KINGS AND QUEENS OF SCOTLAND** 82
   British Kings of Strathclyde 83
   Kings of the Picts 84
   The House of Fergus and Loarn 85
   The House of Dunkeld 91
   The House of Stewart 103

7 **KINGS AND QUEENS OF ENGLAND**   **114**
    The House of Normandy and Blois   115
    The House of Anjou (Plantagenet) Part I   129
    The House of Anjou (Plantagenet) Part II   146
    The House of Lancaster   152
    The House of York   162
    The House of Tudor   170

8 **KINGS AND QUEENS OF GREAT**
    BRITAIN   **188**
    The House of Stuart   189
    The House of Hanover   209
    The House of Saxe-Coburg-Gotha   229
    The House of Windsor   236

    INDEX   **250**

1. ANCIENT BRITISH KINGS AND QUEENS

Elaborate burials hint at paramount chiefs in Britain as much as 4700 years ago. But our first clear proofs of kings in Britain are the Romans' 2000-year-old accounts of contemporary male and female rulers of Iron Age British tribes. These were migrants from mainland Europe who spoke Celtic tongues akin to modern Gaelic, Irish, and Welsh, and used coins based on those of Greece and Rome. After the Roman invasions, begun in 55 BC, certain British monarchs became the Romans' submissive client kings.

Here are brief details of some major Celtic British tribes and monarchs. Most names are romanized, and dates are scarce.

Atrebates. This tribe emerged in what are now Hampshire and Sussex, and became allies of the Romans. **Commius**, its likely founder, had fought Julius Caesar in Gaul (France) and fled to Britain about 50 BC. His sons **Eppillus**, **Tincommius** (recognized by Augustus c15 BC), and **Verica** divided his kingdom, issued Roman-type coins, and used the Roman title *Rex* ('king'). Having lost Calleva (Silchester) to Cunobelinus, Verica fled his remnant of territory in Sussex and sought help at Rome.

Brigantes. These founded Eboracum (York) and their northern kingdom became the largest in all Britain. Apparently successive rulers included **Volisios**, **Dumnocoveros**, and the pro-Roman (Queen) **Cartimandua**, flourishing about AD 50-69.

Catuvellauni. This expansionist tribe lived in and around what is now Hertfordshire. King **Caswallon** (Julius Caesar's Cassivellaunus) fought rival tribes and became a high king of the British. He united several tribes against the first Roman invasions of 55 and 54 BC and later ruled from Verulamium (St Albans). Successors included **Androco** and **Tasciovanus** (recognized by Augustus c15 BC, died cAD 10), both perhaps sons of Caswallon, and Tasciovanus's son **Cunobelinus** (the Shakespearean Cymbeline) (died about AD 43). This ally of the Romans ruled from Camulodonum (Colchester), and his son Adminius fled to Rome even before his father's death. Cunobelinus's other sons **Caradoc** (the Romans' Caractacus or Caratacus) and **Togodumnus** (probably mortally wounded at the Battle of the Medway, 43), resisted Roman onslaughts (AD 43-47), but eventually fled north from Wales to the Brigantes. Their queen, Cartimandua, betrayed him (51) to the Romans who displayed Caradoc and his family in chains at Rome.

Iceni. Their Norfolk and Suffolk lands became a client kingdom under **Prasutagus**. When he died

A Victorian conception of Boudicca and her daughters, by Westminster Bridge since 1902.

(AD 60), Roman troops seized his lands and daughters, provoking rebellion by his widowed queen **Boudicca** (Boadicea). Joined by the Trinovantes, her forces took Londinium (London) before suffering a major defeat. She killed herself by poison (61). Hers was the last really dangerous native revolt in Roman Britain.

Regni. Formerly subordinate to the Atrebates, this tribe's centre was Noviomagnus Regnensium (Chichester, Sussex). **Cogidubnus** or **Cogidumnus** (mid 1st century AD), a 'client king' of the Romans, styled himself legate of the emperor in Britain and, after about 75, built a vast palace at nearby Fishbourne.

2. ROMAN AND ROMANO-BRITISH RULERS

Roman rule of Britain, following major summer raids by Julius Caesar in 55 and 54 BC, began in AD 43 with the Emperor **Claudius I's** invasion. Claudius himself paid a triumphal 16-day visit to his new province. Roman rule eventually embraced England, Wales, and much of Scotland (where in 84 the province's 11th governor Agricola defeated 30,000 Caledonians under Calgacus or Galgacus at Mons Graupius, near ?Aberdeen)), but the core of Roman Britain was the rich farmland of the south-east.

Roman emperors ruled Britain as a province (after 197 as two provinces and after 296 as four) under Roman governors (49 are known, up to AD 242)-with full civil and military powers. Early on these rulers tolerated British client kings like those mentioned on the preceding pages.

Hadrian (reigned 117-138, visited 122), **Antoninus Pius** (reigned 138-161, built the Antonine Wall), and **Septimius Severus** (reigned 193-211; visited and campaigned, with his son Caracalla 208-11)) were among several Roman emperors who visited Britain or struck coins with a British emphasis. Severus died at York (4 Feb 211) and his palace may recently have been discovered there.

One reason Severus came to Britain was because the outlying province had become a powerful enough base for its governor **Clodius Albinus** (192-7) to proclaim himself emperor – until defeated and killed by Severus near Lyons.

Albinus was the first of no fewer than eight Roman
emperors proclaimed in Britain. During the
Empire's near 3rd-century collapse Britain formed
part of the regional Gallic Empire of six successive
usurper emperors (259-73).

   Aurelian restored central control in 274, but in
287, the rebel naval commander of the *Classis
Britannica* and probable main architect of the new
Saxon Shore coastal forts, **Marcus Aurelius
Carausius** proclaimed a British Empire, including
Boulogne and other cross-Channel areas until 293.
He ruled until murdered in 293 by his finance
minister and successor **Caius Allectus**. In 296 the
junior Emperor **Constantius Chlorus I** invaded,
killed Allectus and restored legitimate imperial
authority. Constantius' son **Constantine the Great**
was proclaimed emperor at York after his father's
death there (25 July 306). After Constantine
reunited the Empire during the longest reign since
Augustus, his son **Constans** paid Britain a winter
visit in 342/3. Constans may have built the Saxon
Shore fort of Pevensey. In 383 **Magnus Maximus**,
perhaps victorious against the Picts (382), removed
much of Britain's garrison to pursue the purple in
Gaul. Theodosius I the Great restored central
authority for the last time in 388.

   By 400 attacks from Scotland, Ireland, and
northern Europe were sapping the province's
defences, already undermined by troop
withdrawals and Hadrian's Wall's abandonment.
On the last day of 406 Rome's Rhine frontier
collapsed before a barbarian migration across the

frozen river into Gaul. Britain's remaining legions
were withdrawn to Boulogne by **Constantine III**
(proclaimed by his troops a century after his
namesake and supposed ancestor) to support his
usurping imperial claims and intervention in Gaul
(407-11). In 410 the legitimate Emperor Honorius,
himself at bay behind Ravenna's marshes, wrote to
Britain's cities telling them they were on their own.
In 446 Britons made a final vain appeal for Roman
help as the Western Empire crumbled.

The next century and a half constitute the
impenetrable Dark Ages, especially from a
Romano-British viewpoint. Local romanized kings
appear to have replaced the late imperial four-
province structure. The supreme military post of
Dux Britanniarum, created after 296 and based at
York, may have continued in the new role of
temporarily uniting local British forces against the
invading Saxons, Angles, Jutes, Frisians, Franks,
Picts, Scots and Irish.

Twentieth century scholarship sees this as the
role of **Ambrosius Aurelianus** and his possible son
Artorius (Arthur), but the task of late Roman
cavalry commander need not exclude kingship or
indeed emperorship. According to one of the few
reliable and early sources (Bede in the 7th
century), Ambrosius' parents, killed by Saxons,
were of royal birth and title. Ambrosius apparently
won a first victory over the Angles about 493. The
last and most decisive of Arthur's twelve victories
over the Saxons was Mount Badon, usually dated
about 516 and identified with sites in Wiltshire and

Dorset. Artorius is said to have died in a typical Romano-British civil war at the Battle of Camlan(n) in 537, but Mount Badon checked the Saxons for 40 years.

One of Artorius' battles has been located at Cat Coit Celidon in southern Scotland, a reminder that Romano-British kingdoms also existed in the north spanning the two Roman walls and including the old border tribes. Rheged, focused on Carlisle and the Solway Firth, was one of these kingdoms. Its last rulers **Urien** and **Owain** fought the Northumbrian Angles until the 590s. They were descendants of **Old Coel the Splendid** (Old King Cole of nursery rhyme fame) who may have held sway in the entire lowland frontier zone during the early 5th century. At the Lothian core of this area was the British Kingdom of Gododdin, eventually annexed by Northumbria in the mid-7th century. The last British kingdom in this region, and perhaps Coel's neighbour, was Strathclyde (see separate king list) which survived over half a millenium of vicissitudes to be peacefully incorporated into Scotland (c1016).

3. ANGLO-SAXON MONARCHIES

After formal Roman rule in Britain collapsed in AD 410, shadowy Romano-British rulers briefly reigned in early Dark Age England. Soon, though, they suffered onslaughts from fierce northern tribesmen. One victim was a southern British overlord or vortigern whose title is remembered as his name. About AD 450 **Vortigern** reputedly imported Saxon mercenaries, but these became the spearhead for invading Germanic groups. Recorded as Angles, Saxons, and Jutes, they included also Frisians and Franks.

These incomers from what are now the Netherlands, West Germany, France, and Denmark gradually drove British rulers out of England, despite lengthy and often successful resistance by such semi-legendary kings as **Arthur** or Artorius Rex. The invaders, in time collectively called Anglo-Saxons or English, set up hundreds of petty states. Archaeological, place-name, and other very recent research suggests that early Anglo-Saxon England held as many as 1000 statelets, mostly only 15-40 square miles in area, under different chieftains by AD 550. As strong statelets swallowed neighbours the number dwindled to around 250 within 70 years and down to about 40 by 680. Seven major Anglo-Saxon kingdoms, the so-called Heptarchy of East Anglia, Essex, Kent, Mercia, Northumbria, Sussex, and Wessex, came to dominate the rest. Anglo-Saxon kings claimed the war god Woden as their ancestor. They had special rights to rent and

Woden, God of War, ancestor of all Anglo-Saxon
dynasties except Essex. This late 12th century
depiction has his mythical sons representing
(clockwise from bottom left) Kent, Mercia, East
Anglia, Wessex, Northumbria and Sussex.

certain services, granted land to followers, and bequeathed the crown to a son, with the approval of advisers making up a council called the *Witan*. At times one king became *Bretwalda*, or overlord of all the rest. But true unity emerged only in the 10th century, under the Kings of Wessex.

Names, dates, and achievements of many early rulers in the Heptarchy remain conjectural.

Kings of Kent

Tradition enshrined in the 9th century monastic *Anglo-Saxon Chronicle* claims Kent as the first Anglo-Saxon kingdom, founded in south-east England soon after AD 450. Other evidence points to two Romano-British created early Kentish kingdoms centered on Rochester and Canterbury respectively. By the 590s the 700-square mile East Kent realm had absorbed the smaller Medway state.

Vortigern, a British king of southern Britain, allegedly invited mercenaries from Jutland (western Denmark or more probably the Rhineland) to help him fight off savage northern Picts. Led by the brothers **Hengest** and **Horsa** who landed at Ebbsfleet (near Ramsgate), the so-called Jutes soon established settlements in Kent despite Horsa's early death in battle at Aegelsthrep (Aylesford, near Maidstone). Then they drove out the British, and formed their own kingdom.

By 600 Kent had become the first Christian and reputedly the most powerful of all English kingdoms. Its capital Canterbury was the seat of England's senior archbishop. But Mercia dominated Kent from the middle 700s until 825 when Wessex gained control. Kentish kings descended from Hengest's son **Aesc** (Oisc) gained the dynastic name of Oiscingas. Some names and dates are doubtful.

Hengest (reigned about 455-488) was the first Jutish King of Kent.

Aesc (Oisc) (reigned about 488-512).

Octa (reigned about 512-540).

Eormenric (reigned about 540-560).

Ethelbert (Aethelbert) I (reigned about 560 to 24 Feb 616). He became paramount king of all England south of the River Humber. Before 589 he married Bertha, Christian daughter of his cross-Channel neighbour the Frankish King Charibert, and received St Augustine's 597 mission from Rome (landed at Ebbsfleet) which made Canterbury the centre of Christianity in southern England and Ethelbert the first baptized Anglo-Saxon king. Buried in the new Monastery of SS Peter and Paul, Canterbury.

Eadbald (reigned 24 Feb 616-640) who temporarily renounced Christianity and married his stepmother before taking Emma, daughter of Frankish King Theudebert II of Austrasia, as his queen.

Earconbert (reigned 640 to 14 July 664). He married Sexburga, daughter of King Anna of East Anglia.

Egbert (Ecgberht) I (reigned 14 July 664 to July 673). He ruled Kent and Surrey.

Hlothere (reigned July 673 to 6 Feb 685), younger brother of Egbert I, jointly with **Suaebhard** of Essex from about AD 676). Early on he faced King Ethelred of Mercia's invasion and, after issuing an extant law code, died of wounds fighting the South Saxons brought in by his nephew Eadric.

Eadric (reigned 685-686 or 687, jointly with the East Saxon **Suaebhard**), courtesy of the South Saxons.

Oswini (reigned 688-690, jointly with **Suaebhard**).

Wihtred (reigned 690 to 23 Apr 725, jointly with **Suaebhard** to 692). A powerful monarch, he married (1) Cynegyth, (2) Ethelburga, (3) Werberga and issued a law code.

Ethelbert (Aethelberht) II (reigned 23 Apr 725-762, jointly with his brother **Eadbert I** 725-748, half-brother **Alric** and Eadbert's son **Eardwulf** from about 747). Ethelbert II was the son of Wihtred and Cynegyth.

Egbert (Ecgberht) II (reigned about 765-780), contemporary with Charlemagne. Lost the Battle of Otford (776) to the Mercians.

Ealhmund (subking under Offa of Mercia 784). He was a son of Eafa of Wessex who married a daughter of Ethelbert II.

Eadbert II Praen (reigned 796-798) who seized the throne only to be defeated and captured by Coenwulf who made his own brother **Cuthred** (died 807) the sovereign, the first to leave a coin image. His successors **Coelwulf** and **Beornwulf** reigned a few years.

Egbert (Ecgberht) III was Egbert of Wessex, who expelled King Baldred and absorbed Kent after Egbert defeated its Mercian overlords in 825.

Kings of Sussex

The South Saxons' kings remain obscure. Records name **Aelle (Ella)** as the kingdom's founder. Traditionally landing in AD 477, he conquered the coastal strip of Sussex with the capture of

Pevensey's Roman fort (491) and supposedly
became the first *Bretwalda* (overlord among the
Anglo-Saxon kings); but overlordship seems an
unlikely concept at a time when we now know
England lay split up among scores of petty states.
Cissa reportedly succeeded his father Aelle about
AD 514 and gave his name to Chichester ('Cissa's-
ceaster'), the royal capital.

The South Saxons receive no further *Anglo-
Saxon Chronicle* mention until 607. King Wulfhere
of Mercia asserted his supremacy in 661. Bishop St
Wilfred of York converted the South Saxons, the
last formally pagan kingdom, in 681-6 while King
Ethelwalh ruled.

Ethelwalh (reigned before 685) received the Isle of
Wight from Wulfhere of Mercia and in turn gave
Wilfrid the bisopric of Selsey. Ethelwald was killed
by the Wessex prince Caedwalla (Cadwalla)who
took the Isle of Wight from its King Arwald only
to be ousted by Earldormen Berthun and Andhun.

Berhtun (reigned 685-686) killed invading Kent.

Cadwalla (Caedwalla) of Wessex (reigned about
686-688). His church land grant near Farnham of
688 first mentions Surrey.

Nothelm (reigned in 692) made a land charter to
his sister.

Nunna (reigned about 710-725), kinsman of Ine of

Wessex, made a land grant to the Bishop of Selsey, and his charters of c714-20 first formally mention Sussex.

Aldwuf (reigned about 765) made a land grant.

Osmund (reigned c765-770) land grant including one witnessed by Offa of Mercia who annexed the kingdom around 772. In 825 Sussex submitted to Egbert of Wessex.

Kings of Essex

East Seaxe, the East Saxons' kingdom, probably embraced the counties of Essex and Middlesex, with London as capital. It absorbed such tiny statelets as Hrotha's the Rodings (close to the Roman Road NW of Chelmsford) and the Romano-British Great Chesterford (on the Roman Road south of Cambridge) by about AD 550. Essex remained relatively small and unimportant, dominated by Mercia during the 8th century, and absorbed by Wessex in 825. The king list may omit whole generations. The dynasty claimed descent from the war god Seaxneat, not Woden.

Aescwine (reigned about 527-587). He supposedly founded the kingdom of Essex and was contemporary with the Byzantine-Roman Emperor Justinian (527-565).

Sledda (reigned about 587-before 604). He married Ricole (Ricula), sister of Ethelbert I of Kent.

Saebert (reigned before 604-about 616). He embraced Christianity and was baptized. Essex is first mentioned in this reign. His three sons succeeded, **Sexred**, **Saeward** (both reigned about 616-617) and one unnamed, but all died fighting the West Saxons after expelling Mellitus, first Bishop of London.

Sigeberht I the Little (reigned about 617-before 653).

Sigeberht II the Good (reigned about 653-660). Sigeberht's baptism marked a return to Northumbrian-sponsored Christianity after a generation of paganism.

Swithhelm (reigned about 660-665).Sponsored by King Ethelwald of East Anglia at his baptism by St Cedd.

Sighere (Sigheard) (reigned about 665-683, jointly with his uncle **Sebbi**). He married St Osyth of Mercia.

Sebbi (Sebbe) (reigned about 665-695, jointly with his nephew **Sighere** to about 683). Abdicated to take monastic vows in London. Buried at Old St Paul's.

Sigeheard (reigned about 695-before 709, jointly with his brother **Swafred**). The latter (with Offa below) visited Rome in 709. Middlesex is first mentioned in his reign (704).

Offa (reigned in 709), son of Sigeheard

Saelred (reigned 709-746), descended from Sigeberht the Good. Ethelbald of Mercia granted privileges to the port of London (c730) in this reign which ended in violent death.

Swithred (reigned 746-after 758), grandson of Sigeheard, ruled from Colchester.

Sigeric (reigned 758-798). Abdicated.

Sigered (reigned 798-825). He conceded the kingdom to Egbert of Wessex.

Kings of East Anglia

The Kingdom of the East Angles comprised Norfolk and Suffolk (lands of the north and south people) and part of Cambridgeshire. Kings were called Wuffings after **Wuffa**, the first known East Anglian monarch.

East Anglian kings reportedly included one overlord (*Bretwalda*) of the Anglo-Saxons,

Redwald, but some kings are unknown. From about 790 until 825 East Anglia acknowledged Mercian hegemony before yielding to that of Wessex. On 20 November 870 invading Danes killed the last Anglo-Saxon East Anglian king and control passed to a Danish king, **Guthrum**. In the early 900s East Anglia accepted rule by Edward the Elder of Wessex, and East Anglia became part of England. Here are brief details of Anglo-Saxon kings (some are unknown).

Wuffa (reigned about 571-578). He is considered the first King of East Anglia.

Tytila (reigned about 578-593).

Redwald (Raewald) (reigned about 593-617). Converted to Christianity in Kent, but lured back to paganism by his wife, he supposedly became the fourth *Bretwalda* (overlord among Anglo-Saxon kings), and helped Edwin win the Northumbrian throne (617). The magnificent Sutton Hoo (pagan) ship burial (near Ipswich in Suffolk), four miles from the royal residence at Rendlesham, may commemorate his death.

Eorpwald (Earpwald) (reigned about 617-627). Son of Redwald and converted a Christian by King Edwin of Northumbria but killed by the pagan Ricberht who for a time kept out his half-brother.

Sigeberht (Siegeberht) (reigned about 631-634),

half-brother of Eorpwald. Founded the Dunwich bishopric for St Felix and built a monastery at Burgh Castle, an old Roman fort.

Ecgric (reigned about 634-635), a kinsman of the former who took over when Sigeberht became the first Anglo-Saxon monarch to retire as a monk. King and ex-King were killed in Penda of Mercia's invasion.

Anna (reigned about 633-654). This devout Christian son of Ine, apparently installed by Penda, fathered two saintly daughters and two who married kings. Like his two predecessors he was killed fighting Penda of Mercia.

Ethelhere (Aethelhere) (reigned 654), younger brother of Anna, was killed in the Battle of the Winwaed fighting for Penda of Mercia.

Ethelwold (Aethelwald) (reigned 654-about 663), youngest brother of Anna.

Aldwulf (reigned 663-713), son of Ethelhere and the Northumbrian Princess Hereswith of Deira. Three of his daughters may have been abbesses.

Aelfwald (Alfwold) (reigned 713-749), client of Mercia from c740.

Hun Beonna (reigned about 749)

(St) Ethelbert (reigned 792) beheaded by his father-in-law King Offa of Mercia's order and venerated as Hereford Cathedral's patron.

Athelstan I (reigned about 828-837), the earliest East Anglian monarch to leave a coin image.

Ethelweard (reigned about 837-850)

Silver penny of Edmund

(St) Edmund (Eadmund) (born about 840; reigned about 855-20 Nov 870). East Anglia's last Anglo-Saxon king, defeated and martyred by Danish invaders at Haegelisdun (near Hoxne, 20 miles SE of Thetford, Suffolk, or at Hellesdon by Norwich). Eventually buried at Beadoricesworth (Bury St Edmunds). Became protector of sailors and St George's predecessor as England's patron saint.

Kings of Mercia

Named from *Merce*, Old English for 'boundary people', Mercia originated as an Anglo-Saxon border area east of the Celtic peoples driven west by Anglo-Saxon pressure. Its warlike kings eventually won lands bounded south and north by the rivers Thames and Humber and east and west by East Anglia and Wales.

Annexations by AD 700 included Wocingas (a West Surrey statelet in the Woking-Chertsey area founded by Wocca before 550) and the Anglian Hwicce kingdom. From a late 6th century 400-square mile Winchcombe Cotswold base (NE of Cheltenham), Hwicce had expanded to straddle Gloucestershire, Worcestershire and a third of Warwickshire by the 620s. After an 8th century golden age Mercian power declined.

By 877 almost half Mercia lay under Danish rule, and kings of Wessex completely administratively absorbed the old middle kingdom early in the 10th century. The recorded line of Mercian kings is incomplete. Today, not inappropriately, Mercia's identity is kept alive by the West Mercia Police Force.

Creoda (reigned about 585-593). The first named King of Mercia supposedly descended from Icel, the first continental Angle king to settle in Britain.

Pybba (reigned about 593-606). His family of three sons and two daughters were the foundation of the dynasty.

Ceorl (reigned about 606-626), kinsman of Pybba. His daughter Cwenburga married the dominant King Edwin of Northumbria.

Penda (reigned 632-654/5). A great warrior and virtual anti-hero of Bede's *Ecclesiastical History of the English Nation* (731), this pagan king laid the basis of Mercian supremacy. Before claiming the throne, the young Penda defeated the West Saxons at Cirencester (628) to annex the Kingdom of Hwicce astride the River Severn. With Welsh King Caedwallada of Gwynedd he defeated the previously all-powerful Edwin of Northumbria on Heathfield (Hatfield, Yorks) in 633. Penda defeated and killed the Northumbrian king Oswald at Maserfeld (probably Oswestry, Shrops) on 5 Aug 641 and almost captured the Northumbrian royal citadel of Bamburgh. By 653 he had formed the sub-kingdom of Middle Anglia (East Midlands) for his son **Peada** (died Easter 656) allowing Christianity there. Another son, **Merewald**, ruled newly-occupied Herefordshire. Penda's final invasion of Northumbria ended fatally on the flooding River Winwaed (near Leeds).

Wulfhere (reigned 657-675), younger brother of Peada, led the Mercian overthrow of Northumbrian hegemony in 658 and invaded Wessex, giving King Ethelwalh of Sussex the Isle of Wight. He had to yield Lindsey (Lincolnshire) to Egfrith of Northumbria (661-5).

Ethelred (Aethelred) (reigned 675-704), Wulfhere's brother, won a victory on the Trent to regain Lindsey (679), but abdicated to become a monk.

Coenred (reigned 704-709), eldest son of Wulfhere, gave up the temporal life to go to Rome.

Ceolred (reigned 709-716), son of Ethelred, fought King Ine of the West Saxons.

Ethelbald (Aethelbald) (reigned 716-757), grandson of Penda's brother Eowa (died 641), greatly increased Mercian power and prestige during the dynasty's longest reign, annexing Berkshire from Wessex around 730. He may have built Wat's Dyke against the Welsh before Offa's Dyke. A Worcestershire land charter (736) titles Ethelbald as *Rex Britanniae*. In 749 he reduced church secular financial liablity to paying for fortifications and bridges' upkeep. Murdered by retainers at Seckington, Warwickshire and buried at Repton monastery, Derbyshire.

Beonred (reigned 757).

Offa (reigned 757-796). Descended from Penda's youngest brother, he restored Mercian mastery of all England south of the River Humber. He issued the first major royal coinage (millions of silver pennies minted), compiled influential laws, and built Offa's Dyke, a 120-mile long earthwork protecting Mercia from Welsh attacks, made a trade treaty with Charlemagne (796) and established Lichfield archbishopric. Married to Queen Cynethryth (coin portraits). Two of their four daughters wed client kings.

Ethelbald visits St Guthlac at Crowland Abbey, Lincs
716, from a 12th century MS

Egfrith (reigned 796) only survived his father 141
days having co-ruled since 787.

Coenwulf (reigned 796-821),descended from
Penda's youngest brother. His c814-20 land charter
to Bishop Deneberht first mentions
Worcestershire.

Ceolwulf I (reigned 821-823), brother of the
preceding but deposed.

Beornwulf (reigned 825) defeated by Egbert of
Wessex and then killed by the East Angles.

Ludeca (Ludecan) (reigned 827) killed in battle along with five earls.

Wiglaf (reigned 827-840) expelled by Egbert of Wessex (829) but regained the throne next year. Northamptonshire first mentioned in his land grants of 833. Buried at Repton monastery, Derbyshire.

Beorhtwulf (Berthulf) (reigned 840-852) held a council at Benington, Herts (850) when Viking fleet reported in Thames.

Burgred (reigned 852-874) married Ethelswith, daughter of Ethelwulf of Wessex, and with the latter subjected North Wales. Twice made treaties with the Viking Great Army (868 and 872) only to be driven by it from Repton to exile in Rome.

Ceolwulf II (reigned 874-c880). The last Mercian king was a Danish Viking choice to rule the unannexed but subordinate western half of the English kingdom. He was deposed.

Kings of Northumbria

Northumbria's name comes from *Nortanhymbre*, the Old English for 'people north of the River Humber'. Northumbria emerged after AD 600 from the fusion of two smaller states, Bernicia (roughly Northumberland) and Deira (roughly Humberside) with kings traced back to the mid-sixth century. Bernicia's stronghold of Bamburgh was captured by the Saxon **Ida** in 547. Both royal houses persisted, Ida's son **Aelle** ruling in Deira (c560-88) while another son **Ethelric** ruled Bernicia (568-72) after his father, but Bernicia's supplied most kings of Northumbria. Inland from Bamburgh is the 1950s-excavated 7th century royal palace of Yeavering in the Cheviots, built within an earlier British regal centre.

This kingdom passed its military peak in 685, but by 800 had won international renown for scholars including the historian-monk Bede, who made Northumbria and especially its southern capital York, a great centre of religious and secular learning and art. At its greatest extent, Northumbria covered all land south of the Firth of Forth and north of the Mersey and Humber. In 866/7 the Danish Great Army smashed the old kingdom. There were later attacks by Scandinavians and Scots, and by the mid-10th century kings of Wessex made Northumbria part of England. Most later Northumbrian kings are known by little more than their names.

Ethelfrith) (Aethelfrith) (reigned in Bernicia about 592-616 as son of the third of Ida's six sons). He seized Deira in 604-5 and defeated Aidan, King of the Scots at Daegsastan (603) in the upper Tyne valley. He also captured Chester from the Welsh

(613). Thrice married, he had seven sons and a daughter.

Edwin (reigned 616-633). This Deiran gained power over Bernicia when his and King Redwald of East Anglia's troops killed Ethelfrith in battle on the River Idle. Edwin became the fifth *Bretwalda* (overlord among Anglo-Saxon kings). He annexed Lindsey (Lincs), the Isle of Man, and the British Kingdom of Elmet (the upper Humber area). The Northumbrian also married Princess Ethelburga of Kent, embraced Christianity (627) and died fighting on 12 Oct 633 at Hatfield Chase (Yorks) against Welsh and Mercians who then burnt Yeavering Palace.

Eanfrith (reigned 633-634). With his reign the Bernician eldest son of Ethelfrith regained control of Bernicia. He married a Pictish princess, but was killed by the Welsh king Caedwalla.

(St) Oswald I (born c605; reigned 634 to 5 Aug 641), brother of Eanfrith and refugee in the Hebrides during Edwin's reign, he became sixth *Bretwalda* as well as the first canonized Anglo-Saxon king. Oswald gave Bishop Aidan Lindisfarne island near Bamburgh. He married Princess Cyneburg of Wessex (and their son Ethelwald ruled Deira c651-4) and died fighting Penda of Mercia. His feast day is 5 August.

Oswy (Oswin) (born c602, reigned 641 to 15 Feb 670). This brother of Oswald, after 13 years ruling Bernicia in Penda's shadow, formally united Deira and Bernicia. He annexed Mercia (until 658), conquered much of southern Scotland (Rheged and Gododdin) and became seventh *Bretwalda*. His secular supremacy was matched by his presiding at the crucial ecclesiatical Synod of Whitby (664). By two wives and a mistress, Oswy had four sons and three daughters, two of whom married kings; Alchfled being sufficient inducement to persuade Peada of Mercia to become Christian.

Egfrith (reigned 15 Feb 670 to 20 May 685), son of Oswy by Eanfled of Deira. He drove the Mercians from Lindsey (674), but lost it and a brother killed in 679, being forced back over the Humber. The Picts destroyed him and his army at Nechtansmere near Forfar, Angus, deep in Scotland.

Aldfrith (Alfrid) (reigned 685-704), the son of Oswy's mistress Fina, eschewed war for learning and cultural pursuits.

Osred I (reigned 704-716), son of Aldfrith, died violently.

Coenred (reigned 716-718), contemporary with the failure of the great Arab siege of Constantinople.

Osric (reigned 718-729)

Ceolwulf (reigned 729-737), brother of Coenred and dedicatee of Bede's *Ecclesiastical History*, but temporarily deposed the same year (731) and died a monk in 760.

Eadbert (reigned 737-758), cousin of Ceolwulf, fought a Pictish war (740) annexing part of Ayrshire and, allied to the Picts, temporarily took Dumbarton, capital of the British Strathclyde kingdom (756). His brother Egbert was the first Archbishop of York (735-66) and he himself abdicated for the monastic life.

Oswulf (reigned 758-759), son of the preceding and slain by his own household.

Ethelwald Moll (reigned 759-765) defeated a rebel Oswin but was probably compelled into a monastery.

Alchred (Alhred) (reigned 765-774) sent envoys to the newly ruling Charlemagne (768), but was deposed and fled to the Picts.

Ethelred (Aethelred) I (reigned 774-778 and 790-796), son of Ethelwald Moll, expelled after having three high-reeves (sheriffs) killed, but made a comeback in 790 until murdered at Corbridge by Hadrian's Wall.

Elfwald I (reigned 778-788), murdered by Sicya.

Osred II (reigned 788-790), son of Alchred and nephew of the preceding, killed by Ethelred I.

Osbald (reigned 796). Expelled after only 27 days.

Eardwulf (reigned 796-807/8 and 809). Twice recalled from exile.

Elfwald II (reigned 808/9)

Eanred (reigned 809-841), son of Eardwulf, did homage to Egbert of Wessex (827).

Ethelred II (reigned 841-850), son of Eanred, killed.

Osberht (reigned 850-863) Expelled.

Ella (Aelle) (reigned 863-March 867). Apparently slew the Viking Ragnar Lombrok and drew down the wrath of his sons and the Great Army on Northumbria. Joined with Osberht and regained York (lost Nov 866), but both lost their lives and army in a climactic battle with the Norsemen.

Egbert I (reigned 867-872). Viking-installed ruler of Bernicia, died 873.

Ricsig (reigned 872-876) as above.

Egbert II (reigned 876-878). The last Viking-puppet ruler.

Kings of Wessex

Saxon invaders reputedly founded Wessex (the
Kingdom of the West Saxons) about AD 494.
Wessex was centred on what all became by the late
10th century the southern English counties of
Dorset, Hampshire, Somerset, and Wiltshire.
Between AD 519 and 954 Kings of Wessex,
descended from its founder **Cerdic**, absorbed the
other Anglo-Saxon kingdoms. Here are brief
details of West Saxon kings up to **Edward the
Elder** the last whose rule did not embrace all
England. Major kings receive more detailed
treatment than the rest.

Cerdic (reigned 519-534) recorded as the first King
of Wessex. After fighting ashore from five ships at
Cerdices ora (? near Southampton) with his son
Cynric in 494, he defeated and killed the British
King Natanleod (508) and at Charford, Hants
(519). Despite apparent defeat at Mount Badon he
later captured the Isle of Wight (530).

Cynric (reigned 534-560) extended Wessex beyond
Hampshire, fighting the Britons at Salisbury (552)
and Barbury (556).

Ceawlin (reigned 560-591), son of Cynric, advanced
north of the Thames and was reputedly the second
Bretwalda or overlord among southern Anglo-
Saxon kings. He defeated Ethelbert of Kent in 568

and three British kings (Conmail, Condidan and
Farinmail) at Dyrham (577), 7 miles north of Bath
which he captured with Cirencester and
Gloucester. Yet his battle-filled reign ended with
rebellion and death in exile (592-3).

Ceol (reigned 591-597)

Ceolwulf (reigned 597-611), brother of the
preceding, fought the South Saxons in 607.

Cynegils (reigned 611-643) heavily defeated the
British at Beandun (614), failed in his plot to
murder Edwin of Northumbria (626), embraced
Christianity (635), but lost to Penda's Mercia the
Severn valley Kingdom of Hwicce.

Cenwalh (Cenwedh) (reigned 643-672), son of
Cynegils, first married then put away a sister of
Penda, having to flee the brother's wrath (645),
and extended his rule to mid-Somerset. Then
Cenwalh lost Oxfordshire to Mercia, which also
seized the Isle of Wight and much of Hampshire.
Cenwalh accepted baptism during three years' exile
at the court of King Anna of East Anglia. In
Wessex he built the Old Minster, Winchester (648)
and was buried there.

Seaxburgh (reigned about 672-674) succeeded her
husband Cenwalh thus becoming the only known
Saxon queen to reign on her own.

Cenfus (reigned 674), grandson of Ceolwulf.

Aescwine (reigned 674-676), son of the above.

Centwine (reigned 676-685), brother of Cenwalh.

Cadwalla (born c658; reigned 685-688), descended from Ceawlin, the third Wessex king, regained the Isle of Wight but abdicated the throne and died at Rome (20 Apr 688) after Easter baptism by Pope Sergius who buried him in Old St Peter's.

Ine (reigned 688-726), the most powerful Wessex ruler to date. He issued the first West Saxon law code (690-3); fought the Cornish Britons (710); defeated the South Saxons (722 and 725); set up a port at Southampton; founded the monastery at Glastonbury; and established a bishop in Dorset, where West Saxons had defeated the Britons. Abdicated and died on pilgrimage to Rome.

Ethelheard (Aethelheard) (reigned 726-740). His 739 land charter to Bishop Fortherne first mentions Devon.

Cuthred (reigned 740-756) defeated Ethelbald of Mercia at Burford, Oxon (752)

Sigeberht (reigned 756-757) deposed by the *Witan* in Cynewulf's favour. The latter expelled him from Hampshire for murdering an earldorman. Lived in the Weald until a swineherd avenged the nobleman.

Cynewulf (reigned 757-786) ruled in Offa's shadow and lost Berkshire to him (779). Murdered by Cyneheard, Sigeberht's younger brother, at Merton (Oxon) but wounded him and was avenged by his bodyguard of thegns.

Beohrtric (reigned 786-802) married Eadburga of Mercia, King Offa's daughter. The first (three-ship) Viking raid (787) killed his royal official in Dorset.

Silver penny of Egbert

Egbert (Ecgberht) (born 770/80; reigned 802-839). After exile since 789 at Charlemagne's court, Egbert succeeded his cousin and made Wessex the leading kingdom in England, laying a basis for her future unification. His are the earliest-surviving Wessex coins (c825). By the Wansdyke he may have built, Egbert defeated King Beornwulf of Mercia at the Battle of Ellandune (south of Swindon, Wilts) in 825, ending Mercia's power over Wessex and occupying Mercia in 829. Egbert annexed Essex, Kent, Surrey, and Sussex, and his armies crushed Cornish and Danish forces in the south-west (815, at Galford in person 825, and

838), latterly in person at Hengist Down (near Plymouth). Briefly, he ruled all England south of the River Humber, but never conquered Northumbria. His mainly outstanding descendants (by Redburga) would rule England for more than 150 years.

Gold ring of
Ethelwulf

Ethelwulf (Aethelwulf) (born c800; reigned 839-858) ruled Kent for his father from 828, and on accession joined Mercia in prolonged wars against Danish Viking invaders, winning a major battle at Ockley in Surrey (851), and forging marriage alliances with Mercia and the West Franks. Ethelwulf's gold ring can be seen in the British Museum. His younger brother **Athelstan** ruled Sussex, Surrey and Kent (839-c51). On returning with his fifth son Alfred from a pilgrimage to Rome (856), Ethelwulf was made to share the throne with his son Ethelbald, the first of four in succession who became King of Wessex.

Ethelbald (born c834; reigned 858-860) married his father's widow and his stepmother Judith (daughter of King Charles the Bald of the Franks). Buried at Sherborne Abbey, Dorset.

Ethelbert (Aethelbald) (born c836; reigned 860-865) ruled Kent (851-60) before his accession. The Danes destroyed Winchester (860) and ravaged Kent (865). Buried at Sherborne Abbey, Dorset.

Ethelred (Aethelred) I (born c840; reigned 865 to Apr 871) , fourth son of Ethelwulf, known as St Ethelred for his piety, backed Mercia (868) in opposing eastern England's Danish invaders, and with Alfred fought eight battles (871) against Danish invaders of Wessex. Died of wounds received in the Battle of Merton (Oxon) and buried at Wimborne Minster, Dorset.

Silver penny and jewel of Alfred

Alfred (Aelfred) the Great (born Wantage, Berks c849; reigned Apr 871 to 26 Oct 899). Most famous of all West Saxon kings, Alfred saved England from its Danish invaders, laid a basis for national unity, and promoted learning. Architect of his brother Ethelred's victory at Ashdown (8 Jan 871), Berks, Alfred was almost overwhelmed by a Jan 878 Danish winter onslaught on Wessex; he retreated into the Somerset Athelney marshes,

gathered an army, and crushed the Danes at the
Battle of Ethandune (near Edington, Wilts, May
878). Later, he captured London (886) and
repulsed a great Danish seaborne invasion (892-6).
Alfred built power by raising 30 forts (burghs),
probably including Oxford and Hastings,
reorganizing the *fyrd* (army), and founding the first
long-term English navy. All outside Danish-ruled
England recognized Alfred as king.

Alfred was a wise and just ruler. He introduced
a major new law code and split parts of Mercia into
shires. Boyhood visits to Rome (853 and 855) had
helped him become a devout Christian and scholar.
He invited foreign scholars to visit his court,
translating five major books from Latin, and
encouraging the reading and writing of English.
Alfred married (867) Ealhswith of the Gaini
(Elswitha, died 902), a descendant of Mercian
kings, and was buried at Winchester Old Minster.
They had two sons and three daughters.Their
descendants ruled England until 1066.

Edward (Eadweard) the Elder (born 870; reigned
26 Oct 899 to 17 July 924, died Farndon-on-Dee,
Cheshire) asserted his power over most of
England. Inheriting Wessex from his father Alfred
and killing a Danish-backed claimant Ethelwald
(902), Edward conquered all the Danish Five
Boroughs (Leicester, Stamford, Nottingham,
Derby and Lincoln) south of the Humber (917-
919), building 11 new forts there (eg Manchester
919). He inherited an already closely-allied Mercia

Silver penny of
Edward the Elder

after the death of its ruler, Edward's sister
Ethelfleda (Aethelflaed) (12 June 918). He also
subdued Northumbria (920). His sons Athelstan
(two children by his first mistress Egwina or
Ecgwyn); eight children by his second wife Elfleda;
and Edmund and Edred (by his third wife Edgifu
or Eadgifu) all became kings. Six of his daughters
married kings or dukes in France, Germany,
Bohemia and York. Edward was buried at
Winchester New Minster.

Kings of England

While England's regional Anglo-Saxon monarchs
often recognized a single overlord, no one king
directly ruled all England until the 10th century.
Historians accordingly reject the claims for the
West Saxon King Egbert (who never held
Northumbria), and Edward the Elder (whose
direct rule did not embrace the Danish Kingdom of
York). Egbert's descendant Athelstan (reigned
924-939) is generally held to be the first King of all
England. After Athelstan, West Saxon kings

descended from Egbert ruled England for about 75
years until displaced by the Danes Sweyn
Forkbeard and his son Canute, and for 24 years
after the Danish interval. England's West Saxon
kings fought with varying success to maintain
power, but their rule saw the emergence of
national laws and institutions and a monastic
reformation.

ATHELSTAN (AETHELSTAN, ETHELSTAN)
924-939
Authority King of England
Parents Edward the Elder and Egwina (Ecgwyn),
their first born
Born about 895
Succeeded to throne 17 July 924
Crowned Kingston-upon-Thames, Surrey 4 Sept
925
Reigned 15 years, 102 days
Died 27 Oct 939
Buried Malmesbury Abbey, Wilts
Unmarried
Key facts He became the first Saxon king with
effective control of all England (except Cumbria).
He crushed a Scottish-Viking attack at Brunanburh
(937), where five kings perished, and became at
least in name overlord of Celtic kingdoms in
Cornwall, Scotland, and Wales. He introduced a
national coinage, and passed laws to relieve
poverty and punish theft and corruption. Athelstan
had a corps of clerks that foreshadowed the civil

Silver penny of Athelstan minted at London

service. He married four of his sisters to dukes in France and Holy Roman Emperor Otto I the Great (930).

EDMUND (EADMUND) I 939-946
Nicknames The Deed-Doer, the Magnificent, the Elder
Authority King of England
Parents Edward the Elder and Edgifu, their eldest son
Born 921
Succeeded to throne 27 Oct 939
Reigned Six years, 210 days
Died Pucklechurch, Gloucestershire, 26 May 946
Buried Glastonbury Abbey, Somerset
Married (1) (St) Elfgifu (Aelfgifu) (died 944), by whom he had two sons and (2) Ethelfled (Aethelflaed) of Damerham
Children Edwy (Eadwig) and Edgar
Key facts Having commanded under his half-brother Athelstan at Brunanburgh, Edmund recaptured parts of the Midlands (942) and Northumbria (944) seized by Norse King Olaf Guthfrithson of Dublin (died 942) after Athelstan's death. He secured the Anglo-Scottish border by

subduing Strathclyde (945), handing this to
Malcolm I of Scotland for promised military aid.
Powerful Wessex-born ealdormen brothers ruled
East Anglia and Kent for the King. An Edmund
charter first records Derbyshire. Edmund was
stabbed to death by Leofa, an exiled thief; an
ironic fate when the first Hundred (district) court
originated in his reign.

EDRED (EADRED) 946-955
Authority King of England
Parents Edward the Elder and Edgifu (Eadgifu),
their second son
Born 923
Succeeded to throne 26 May 946
Reigned Nine years, 181 days
Died Frome, Somerset, 23 Nov 955
Buried Winchester Old Minster, Hants
Key facts Despite ill-health,Edred crushed a
northern revolt and made Northumbria a
permanent part of England. When Northumbria
rejected his rule in favour of Eric Bloodaxe of
Norway, Edred ravaged Northumbria (948),
burning Ripon, but secured it only with Bloodaxe's
expulsion and death in 954.Edred supported the
monastic reforms of his chief adviser Dunstan,
Abbot of Glastonbury.

EDWY (EADWIG) 955-959
Nickname The Fair
Authority King of England
Parents Edmund I and Elfgifu, their eldest son
Born about 940
Succeeded to throne 23 Nov 955
Crowned Kingston-upon-Thames, Surrey
Reigned Three years, 313 days
Died 1 Oct 959
Married Elfgifu (Aelfgifu) by 956, his step-mother's daughter
Key facts Eadwig lost control of England north of the River Thames. Succeeding his uncle aged about 15, Edwy quarreled with and exiled the influential church leader Dunstan. In 957 Mercia and Northumbria rejected Edwy as king in favour of Edgar, his younger brother. From then on he controlled only Kent and Wessex.

EDGAR (EADGAR) 959-975
Nicknames The Peaceful, the Peaceable, the Great
Authority King of the English and of the other people living within Britain
Parents Edmund I and Elfgifu, their second son
Born 943 or 944
Succeeded to throne 1 Oct 959
Crowned Bath, Somerset 11 May 973
Reigned 15 years, 280 days
Died 8 July 975
Buried Glastonbury Abbey, Somerset
Married (1) Ethelfled (Aethelflaed), daughter of

Silver penny of Edgar

Edgar holding a palm,
from an 11th century MS
of his 'Monastic
Agreement' (c970)

Earldorman Ordmaer, and (2) Elfrida (Elfthryth,
Aelfthryth), daughter of Earldorman Ordgar
Children Edward (Eadweard) the Martyr (by 1);
Edmund Aethling (died 971) and Ethelred
(Aethelred) II (by 2). By the nun Wilfthryth, his
mistress of 961, he had a daughter St Eadgyth (died
984).
Key facts Edgar's peaceful rule promoted
England's monastic revival, enhanced the crown's
sanctity, and began doubling the realm's mints to
60 starting a six-year cycle of currency issue.

Nobles discontented with rule by his brother
Edwy made Edgar King of Mercia and
Northumbria (957), and Edwy's death made him

king of all England. Edgar reinstated Dunstan who became his chief adviser and Archbishop of Canterbury (961-88). Edgar supported the founding of 40 abbeys, and among six law codes were imposed the first penalties for non-payment of taxes due to the Church. By 970 Wessex-born brother earldormen administered Mercia and East Essex for Edgar. Apart from one campaign against the Welsh King of Gwynedd (c968), Edgar only needed to build and sail fleets to secure his forebears' military successes, receiving homage from the kings of Strathclyde and Scotland (in return for Lothian). After his coronation he was supposedly rowed on the River Dee at Chester by six or eight kings (Malcolm of Strathclyde, Kenneth II of Scotland, Maccus of the Isle of Man and up to five Welsh sovereigns).

(ST) EDWARD (EADWEARD) II 975-978
Nickname The Martyr
Authority King of England
Parents Edgar and Ethelfled, their only child
Born about 963
Succeeded to the throne 8 July 975
Reigned Two years, 253 days
Died Corfe Castle, Dorset, 18 Mar 978
Buried Wareham, Dorset; reburied (980) Shaftesbury Abbey, Dorset
Key facts His brief reign saw a secular landowners' anti-monastic reaction and ended with the teenage king's murder. Edward supported his influential

adviser Archbishop Dunstan, but at two conferences failed to stop widespread expulsions of monks and seizures of monastic estates, led by Earldorman Aelfhere of Mercia. Edward was murdered on a visit to his half-brother Ethelred, in a plot (perhaps his step-mother's) that made Ethelred king. Edward became venerated as a martyr (1001)and saint for miracles supposed to occur at his tomb.

ETHELRED (AETHELRED) II 978-1016
Nickname The Unready, 12th century from the Anglo-Saxon *unraed* ('ill-advised')
Authority King of England
Parents Edgar I and Elfrida, their second surviving son
Born about 968
Succeeded to throne 18 Mar 978
Crowned Kingston-upon-Thames, Surrey 11 Apr 978
Reigned 38 years, 36 days
Died London 23 Apr 1016
Buried Old St Paul's Cathedral, London
Married (1) Elfled (Elgifu, Aelfgifu) of Northumbria and (2) Emma of Normandy 1002
Children Edmund II and at least five others (by 1); Edward the Confessor and two others (by 2)
Key facts A militarily ineffective king, Ethelred also failed to buy off Norse invaders who raided England remorselessly from all sides (980 onwards). He issued ten lawcodes and levied taxes to pay the Vikings protection money called

Danegeld (£167,000 from 991). By massacring
Danish settlers throughout England (13 Nov 1002)
Ethelred provoked invasions by the Danish King
Sweyn (1003-6 and 1013) and Thorkell the Tall
(1009-13). Finally Ethelred fled to Normandy
(1013), returning after Sweyn's death early in 1014.
Ethelred's marriage to the daughter of Richard II
the Good, 5th Duke of Normandy, formed an
Anglo-Norman family tie, a basis for the 1066
Norman invasion.

EDMUND (EADMUND) II 1016

Nickname Ironside (for valiant resistance to the
Vikings)
Authority King of the England
Parents Ethelred II and Elfled, their eldest
surviving son
Born before 993
Succeeded to throne 23 Apr 1016
Reigned Seven months (222 days)
Died London 30 Nov 1016
Buried Glastonbury Abbey, Somerset
Married Eadgyth, widow of Sigeferth
Children Edward the Exile (died 1057), Edmund
Key facts The warlike Prince Edmund's efforts to
oppose Canute's late 1015 invasion of Wessex were
negated by Earldorman Edric of Mercia's
treachery. Early in 1016 Edmund laboriously raised
an army but could not hold Northumbria against
Canute. On his father Ethelred's death, London
and *Witan* members resident there chose Edmund

as king while the *Witan* majority at Southampton chose Canute. The Saxon King marched into Wessex and won three of four battles, relieving besieged London but his cause was crippled by Edric's failure to commit his Mercian troops at the Battle of Ashington (Assandun) in Essex, 18 Oct 1016. At Olney (Glos) Edmund and Canute agreed to partition England. A few weeks later Edmund of Wessex died, probably naturally although later sources say he was murdered. His infant sons fled Canute's takeover and settled in Hungary.

(SAINT) EDWARD (EADWEARD) THE CONFESSOR 1042-1066

Authority King of England
Parents Ethelred II and Emma of Normandy, their eldest son
Born Islip, Oxfordshire about 1003
Succeeded to the throne 8 June 1042
Crowned Winchester 3 Apr 1043
Reigned 23 years, 294 days
Died Westminster 5 Jan 1066
Buried Westminster Abbey
Married Edith (Eadgyth) (died 1075), daughter of Godwin (Godwine), Earl of Wessex (active c1020-53), 1043
Children None
Key facts Edward was a saintly but ineffectual king who restored Saxon rule but boosted Norman influence, paving the way for William's conquest.

Edward lived in Norman exile (1013-41) while Danes ruled England. With the death of the last

Edward the Confessor with a model of Westminster Abbey

Danish king, Edward's half-brother Hardecanute, Edward took the throne. But Godwin, Earl of Wessex, really ran the country, marrying his daughter to Edward. After a rift with Godwin, Edward banished Godwin's family (1051-2) and brought Normans into high government positions. This antagonized the English. The Godwins regained power and drove out many of Edward's Norman advisers. In return for Norman support, Edward had apparently promised England's crown to his great-nephew William of Normandy in 1051, but after Godwin's death (1053) Edward relied heavily on Godwin's son and the royal brother-in-law, Harold. The dying monarch allegedly named Harold his successor. Edward founded Westminster Abbey and led a pious, monastic life. He was canonized in 1161.

Edward's burial, from the Bayeux Tapestry

HAROLD II 1066
Authority King of England
Parents Godwin, Earl of Wessex (son of the Sussex thegn Wilnoth Cild) and Gytha, sister of Canute's Danish brother-in-law Ulf, their second son
Born about 1020
Succeeded to the throne 5 Jan 1066
Crowned Westminster Abbey 6 Jan 1066
Reigned Nine months (283 days)
Died Senlac, Sussex 14 Oct 1066
Buried Pevensey seashore, later Waltham Holy Cross Abbey, Essex (his 1060 foundation)
Married (1) Edith (Eadgyth) Swan Neck (in fact a mistress) and (2) Aldgyth (Ealdgyth), widow of Gruffydd ap Llywelyn 1063
Children Four sons and two daughters by (1), and at least one son, Harold, by (2)
Key facts This forceful military leader was effectively the last Saxon king of England and in many senses reigned 13 years not nine months.

Harold, Earl of East Anglia (1044-53) inherited all his father's lands and influence (1053) as Earl of Wessex and Kent dominating Edward the Confessor. He added Hereford to his lands and skilfully crushed Welsh risings by 1063. Shipwrecked and held by Duke William of Normandy about 1064, Harold supposedly secured release by promising to help Duke gain the English crown, but in 1066 claimed the dying Edward had named him his successor. Ignoring claims by Edward's teenage great-nephew Edgar the Atheling (c1050-c1125), Harold had himself declared king but faced invasion by rival claimants Harold III Hardrada of Norway and William of

Harold's crown from his coinage

Harold's coronation, from the Bayeux Tapestry

Normandy. Harold killed Hardrada and Harold's own hostile younger brother Tostig at the Battle of Stamford Bridge outside York (25 Sept 1066). Three days later William invaded Sussex. The victor of Stamford Bridge forced marched south 250 miles in nine days but narrowly lost the all-day Battle of Hastings (14 Oct). Harold died fighting (as did two of his three remaining brothers) cut down by a sword (not, as often said, struck by an arrow). With Harold's death ended England's 600 years of rule by Anglo-Saxon kings. His elder daughter Gytha married King Waldemar of Novgorod (died 1125) and, the younger, Gunhild was a nun at Wilton Abbey (Wilts). The fate of his sons, two of whom landed in North Devon from Ireland during the 1068-9 risings against William, is unknown.

Scandinavian Kings in Britain

Danish and Norwegian Viking raids begun in the late 8th century led to widespread Scandinavian conquests and colonization in the British Isles. King Alfred's Saxon-Danish treaty of 886 left the so-called Danelaw (Danish England) covering much of England north and east of a line from London to the Mersey. During 900-925 Norwegian settlements extended from west of the Pennines to York, a capital and international trading centre. A century later renewed invasions culminated in Canute's Danish dynasty ruling all England for 26 years. In 1042 the throne reverted to a Saxon (Edward the Confessor) and remained in Saxon hands until William of Normandy's invasion of 1066. Here are brief details of some local Scandinavian rulers in England, followed by the Danish kings of England.

NORSE KINGS OF EAST ANGLIA AND YORK (NORTHUMBRIA) 875-954

Guthrum, a Danish army leader since at least 875, attacked Wessex in Jan 878, was defeated by Alfred at Ethandune and made the Treaty of Wedmore. He then became King of East Anglia (in the Danelaw) reigning 880-890. Sponsored by Alfred, Guthrum embraced Christianity at the River Aller in Somerset and issued coins in his baptismal name Aethelstan. Guthrum's son **Eric** reigned until 902. The last Danish King of East Anglia was killed fighting Edward the Elder's Saxons (918).

Halfdan Ragnarson (of Dublin) (reigned 875-883), founder of the Norse Kingdom of Jorvik or York which had 13 Viking rulers in 80 years.

Guthfrith (or Guthred), Danish King of Jorvik or York (reigned 883-895), a Christian convert buried in the Old Minister, York.

Ragnald I (reigned 919-921), a Norse leader from Dublin, became king of the Norse kingdom of York, embracing much of Northumbria.

Sihtric Caoch (of Dublin) (reigned 921-927), Ragnald's successor had been expelled from Dublin (920) by his brother Guthfrith, and married the sister of King Athelstan of England (926).

Guthfrith (of Dublin) brother of Sihtric, was soon expelled by Athelstan and died in Dublin (934). His son Olaf Guthfrithsson, King **Olaf II of Dublin** from 934, joined the great confederation that lost at Brunanburh (937) and died raiding Lowland Scotland (941/2).

Olaf Sihtricsson (of Dublin) (born c920: reigned 941-943) son of Sihtric and known as Olaf the Red, also lost at Brunanburgh but reclaimed Northumbria after Athelstan's death only to be captured by Edmund I. Released, he ousted his cousin Blakare Guthfrithsson to become the longest-reigning King of Dublin (c945-80), the Isle of Man and the Western Isles, and also disputed the York-based kingdom with Eric Bloodaxe.

Ragnald II (reigned 943-944), cousin of the preceding and brother of Olaf Guthfrithsson, was the Saxon-Viking compromise occupant of the throne until Edmund reasserted English direct rule in 944.

Eric (Erik) Bloodaxe, a deposed (934) king of Norway, fled to England and seized Northumbria from Edred (947-8 and 952-4). He may have become Christian and undoubtedly struck a coinage. Eric was killed with his brother and son at Stainmore in an ambush by Edred's army (954) and Northumbria became a permanent part of England.

DANISH KINGS OF ENGLAND

SWEYN (SVEN, SVEIN)
Nickname Forkbeard (*Tiugeskaeg*)
Authority King of Denmark, Norway and England
Parents Harold Bluetooth (Harald Blaatand), King of Denmark and Queen Gunild (probably)
Succeeded to the throne winter 1013
Reigned in England A few weeks
Died Gainsborough, Lincs 3 Feb 1014
Buried London, then Denmark
Married (1) Gunhild (died 992) daughter of Duke Miesko of Poland and (2) Sigrid the Haughty (died 995), widow of King Erik Sersel of Sweden
Children Harold IV of Denmark and Canute the Great by (1); Estrith (Astrid, Astrith) by (2)
Key facts Sweyn I seized Denmark from his father (987) and forged a North Sea empire by conquest and marriage. He attacked Norway, becoming its effective ruler (1000). Sweyn often attacked England from 994, securing protection payments and in 1003-4 avenging the St Brice's Day massacre of Danes (that included his sister Gunhild). In

Aug-Dec 1013 he drove Ethelred II from England and the exhausted English accepted Sweyn as king, but he died after a fall from his horse.

Silver penny of Canute

CANUTE (CNUT, KNUT) 1016-1035
Nicknames The Great, the Wealthy (in his own lifetime)
Authority King of England, Denmark (from 1019), and Norway (after 1028), overlord of the Scots, and perhaps ruler of Dublin
Parents Sweyn Forkbeard and Gunhild of Poland, their younger son
Born about 992
Succeeded to throne 30 Nov 1016
Crowned 1018
Reigned 18 years, 347 days
Died Shaftesbury, Dorset 12 Nov 1035
Buried Winchester Old Minster, Hants
Married (1) Elfgifu (Elfgiva, Aelfgifu) of Northumbria/Northampton, daughter of Earldorman Aelfhere of Deira (an informal liaison) about 1013 and (2) Emma of Normandy (died 1052), widow of Ethelred II, 1017
Children Sweyn, King of Norway, and Harold I Harefoot (by 1) and (by 2) Hardecanute and Gunhild (died 1038)

Canute and Queen Elfgifu present a cross to
Newminster Abbey, Morpeth, Northumberland
c 1016-20

Key facts Canute established a Danish dynasty in England and brought firm but enlightened rule to his North Sea Empire. Building on his father's successes, Canute fought the Saxon King Edmund II to a draw (Oct 1016) and after Edmund's early death, the *Witan* (king's council) acclaimed Canute King of all England. He harshly stamped out or pre-empted resistance by murders and outlawing, but by 1018 made Englishmen earls of Mercia and Wessex.

Canute won renown for able and just rule, spending more time in England than his other realms. He strongly supported the Church (pilgrimage to Rome 1027-8), successfully extracted homage from Scotland (1031), boosted England's Baltic and German trade and prestige, and used force and guile to win or keep power in Scandinavia. The Norse Kingdom of Dublin issued his coins.

HAROLD I 1035-1040
Nickname Harefoot
Authority King of England
Parents Canute and Elfgifu, their second son
Born 1016
Succeeded to the throne 12 Nov 1035
Reigned Four years, 125 days (1035-37 as regent)
Died Oxford 17 Mar 1040
Buried Old Westminster Abbey, then St Clement Dane's, London
Key facts Harold ruled England as Regent (elected

Queen Emma receives her biography from a monk of St Omer, watched by her two sons, the future Kings Hardecanute and Edward the Confessor c1040

at Oxford), with Earl Leofric of Mercia's backing, while his half-brother Hardecanute was busy in Denmark. In 1036 his followers blinded and murdered rival claimant to the throne Alfred the Aetheling (son of Ethelred II) and, although illegitimate, Harold had himself proclaimed King of England (1037). He expelled Hardecanute's mother Emma to exile at Bruges, and repelled Scottish and Welsh invasions.

HARDECANUTE (HARDICANUTE, HARTHACNUT) 1040-1042

Authority King of Denmark and England
Parents Canute and Emma of Normandy, their only son
Born 1018 or 1019
Succeeded to throne 17 Mar 1040
Reigned Two years, 83 days
Died Lambeth, London 8 June 1042
Buried Winchester Old Minster, Hants
Key facts Hardecanute's brief reign was marred by violence and treachery. His half-brother Harold briefly ousted him while Hardecanute established his reign in Denmark (1035-42). On Harold's death, Hardecanute returned to England backed by a large fleet. He incurred unpopularity for acts including throwing Harold's body in a bog, burning Worcester for killing royal tax collectors, and murdering the captured Earl Edwulf of Northumbria (1041). Hardecanute died of a fit while drinking at a wedding feast.

LATER NORSE RULERS IN THE BRITISH ISLES 1079-1329

Scandinavian monarchs no longer ruled England after Hardecanute's death but they continued to be important in the Celtic lands. The Kings of Dublin reigned for a century after the Norman Conquest of England. In the far north the Earls (Jarls) of Orkney and the Isles, whose Viking predecessors had displaced the original Picts during the 9th century, ruled until 1329 under the nominal suzerainty of Norway.

The most remarkable late Norse dynasty of all was founded by **Godfred I Crovan** who captured the Isle of Man in 1079 (reigned till 1095), previously under the Dublin and Orkney rulers (since 990). Godfred's 12 successors ruled this island kingdom until 1265. The seventh King of Man was **Somerled** (1158-64), thane of Argyll and of Irish descent who became the first Lord of the (Western) Isles (c1140-64) by expelling the Norsemen. Somerled's nine male descendants claimed the Hebrides until 1493. The last King of Man, **Magnus II**, died in 1265 and Norway sold the island to Scotland which only gained control after a battle in 1275. From 1333 Edward III continuously ruled England's largest offshore island or rather subcontracted its government to noble families, but the legacy of Godfred's kingdom is reflected in the Manxmen's self-governing crown dependency status to this day.

4. WELSH KINGS AND PRINCES

After Roman rule collapsed, kings and kingdoms emerged in Wales from Celtic tribal groups speaking the Brythonic tongue that would develop into modern Welsh. Welsh kings were military leaders, making war upon each other to win wealth, and exacting payments from their subjects in return for some protection from other warlike kings. Most kings passed on their titles to a son or several sons, but sometimes other relatives would claim the throne.

By war and marriage, powerful kings eventually forged three main units: Gwynedd (at least 37 rulers known, c500-1283) in North Wales; Powys (12 rulers known, 1063-1269) in north-central Wales; and Deheubarth (22 rulers known, 872-1201) in South Wales. During the 9th century kings of Gwynedd spread their power by force and royal marriage, and sometimes dominated all Wales. Meanwhile Welsh kings met varying fortunes resisting Anglo-Saxons, Vikings, and Anglo Normans. By 1200 Welsh kings had been reduced to lords and princes owing homage to the King of England. The last independent Prince of Wales was killed in 1282.

Here are brief details of major Welsh rulers.

Cunedda (about AD 388), a chieftain settled by the British-based and self-proclaimed Roman Emperor Magnus Maximus in North Wales from whom the Kings of Gwynedd claimed descent. Cardigan gets its name from Cunedda's son Ceredig.

Maelgwn Hir (reigned about 517). Christian King of Gwynned based on Deganwy, Cunedda's old stronghold near Conway.

Cadwallon ap Cadfan (died about 625). Christian King of Gwynedd whose gravestone is today in Llangadwaladr Church, Anglesey.

Caedwalla (alias Cadwalader, Cadwallon) (died 634). King of Gwynedd. Allied to King Penda of Mercia he helped defeat and kill King Edwin of Northumbria near Doncaster (633), but lost his own life to Edwin's nephew Oswald at the Battle of Heavenfield near Hadrian's Wall. Oswald then drove out Caedwalla's son Cadwallader.

Merfyn Frych (Merfyn the Freckled) (reigned 825-844). King of Gwynedd who married Nest, the King of Powys' daughter; their son was Rhodri Mawr.

Rhodri Mawr the Great (reigned 844-878) was a king of Gwynedd who resisted Viking attacks (856) and dominated Powys (from 855) and briefly part of Deheubarth (South Wales) by marriage (872) to Angharad, heiress of Greater Ceredigion. Killed in battle with the English Mercians after returning from a Viking-enforced exile in Ireland.

Anarawd (reigned 878-916), son of Rhodri Mawr, shared with his five brothers rule of Rhodri's lands. Allied himself to the Viking King of York, and

raided South Wales, whose kings asked for
protection from Alfred the Great of Wessex.
Anarawd himself paid homage to Alfred, the first
such Welsh submission, and secured English aid
against his brother **Cadell** of Ceredigion (reigned
878-c909).

Hywel Dda the Good (reigned c904-950), Rhodri's
grandson and son of Cadell, briefly united North
and South Wales from 942. By marriage to
Princess Elen, daughter of King **Llywareh ap
Hyfaidd**, he secured the south-western Kingdom of
Dyfed (c904) and ruled southern Welsh kingdoms
later collectively called Deheubarth. He eventually
absorbed Gwynedd and Powys, but also
acknowledged Edward the Elder (918) and
Athelstan of England (928) as overlords. Hywel
made a pilgrimage to Rome (928). He was the only
Welsh ruler to issue a coinage (silver pennies) and
his law code does survive in a 13th century text.

Idwal Foel (Idwal the Bald) (reigned 916-942). Son
of Anarawd killed rebelling against Edmund II of
England. Hywel Dda inherited his Gwynedd
realm.

Iago ap Idwal I (reigned 950-979), son of Idwal Foel
expelled from Gwynedd by Hywel Dda, but won
his way back to the throne against Hywel's son
Owain. Deposed by his son Hywel the Bad.

Owain ap Hywel (reigned c954-988). King of Gwynedd and Deheubarth, retaining the latter kingdom.

Hywel ap Idwal the Bad (reigned 979-985). King of Gwynedd and succeeded by his brother **Cadwallon** (reigned 985-986).

Maredudd ap Owain ('son of Owain') (reigned c986-999), Hywel's grandson, again brought temporary unity from Deheubarth to north and south, but prolonged power struggles set in when he died.

Cynan (reigned 999-1005), Hywel the Bad's son who inherited Gwynedd at Maredudd's death.

Llywelyn ap Seisyll (reigned 1018-1023). Son-in-law of Maredudd by marrying his daughter Angharad, he briefly recovered Gwynedd.

Iago ap Idwal II (reigned 1023-1039). Grandson of the first Iago. His exiled son Cyan married Ragnhildr, daughter of the Norse King Olaf of Dublin and their son was Gruffydd ap Cyan. Iago was contemporary with King **Maredudd ab Edwin** of Deheubarth (1033-5) whose death in battle may be memorialized by the 13ft Carew Cross, Dyfed.

Gruffydd ap Llywelyn ('Griffith son of Llywelyn' ap Seisyll) (reigned 1039 to 5 Aug 1063) conquered Gwynedd and Powys (1039), briefly united all

Wales by annexing Deheubarth (1055). Marrying the daughter of the deposed Earl Aelfgar of Mercia, he ravaged the English border, but Earl Harold Godwinson of Wessex captured his court at Rhuddlan (1062) and Gruffydd's own men took their leader's head to the future last Anglo-Saxon king. Gruffydd's brother **Bleddyn ap Cynfyn** ruled in Powys (1063-75) followed by his three sons and their descendants until 1269.

Gruffydd ap Cynan (b c1055, reigned 1081-1137). Of the Gwynedd royal line, but born in Ireland, he thrice invaded his ancestral realm from 1075. He secured it briefly in 1081 by defeating King **Trahaiarn** of Powys (Bleddyn's cousin) before the Normans captured him. Escaping from Chester, he reconquered Gwynedd, resisting two of William II's campaigns and finally rendered homage to Henry I. His daughter Gwenllian married King **Gruffydd ap Rhys** of Deheubarth.

Rhys ap Tewdwr ('son of Tewdwr') (reigned 1081-1093) secured William I's recognition of his rule of Deheubarth for £40 per annum (1086). Not long after Anglo-Normans overran almost all South Wales and Rhys was killed at Brecheinoc by his own troops. His son **Gruffydd ap Rhys** (1135-1137) and four grandsons carried on the struggle.

Madog ap Maredudd ('son of Maredudd') (reigned 1132-1160). This forceful Prince of Powys thrust its borders east during the English Anarchy, but his son and grandson divided Powys for good.

Owain (Owen) Gwynedd (b c1100, reigned 1137-1170) strengthened his father Gruffydd ap Cynan's North Wales kingdom, advancing into Ceredigion and even to the Dee. Henry II forced a token submission (1157), but Owain united with South Wales rulers to thwart his campaign of 1165. This King of Gwynedd is buried in Bangor Cathedral and his son **Dafydd** (David), who reigned 1170-1194, proved the most durable of his five sons and married Henry II's illegitimate half-sister Emma.

Rhys ap Gruffydd (The Lord Rhys) (b c1133, reigned 1155-1197). Fourth and youngest son of Gruffydd ap Rhys, he succeeded his brother **Madog** as King of Deheubarth in 1155. He skilfully exploited the departure of Norman Marcher barons to Ireland (from 1169) to extend his domains into Dyfed, rebuilding Cardigan and Dinefwr castles. The former place saw an eisteddfod in 1176. Rhys founded Strata Florida Abbey (1164-1294). He is buried in St David's Cathedral with his raven emblem.

Llywelyn ap Iorwerth, Llywelyn the Great ('son of Iorwerth') (born Dolwyddelan Castle, Gwynedd 1173; reigned 1194 to 11 Apr 1240, died Conway, Gwynedd). Prince of Gwynedd and grandson of Owain Gwynedd he defeated his uncle **Dafydd** who had exiled him and reunited the formerly divided

Gwynedd by 1202. From there he dominated other Welsh princes, and in 1205 married Joan (died 1237), illegitimate daughter of King John of England. Weathering John's 1210-11 attempt to clip his wings, he exploited civil war in England, taking all but two royal castles in the south to control Powys (1216). He achieved recognition at Worcester (1218) as Wales' paramount lord. Llywelyn took the one-off and resounding title of Prince of Aberffraw (in Anglesey) and Lord of Snowdon.

David ap Llywelyn (reigned 1240-1246). Second son and widely recognized heir of Llywelyn the Great from 1229 and titled Prince of Wales from 1244. His unexpected death without heirs led to the principality's partition among his elder brother's sons.

Llywelyn ap Gruffydd, Llywelyn the Last ('son of Gruffydd') (reigned 1246 to 11 Dec 1282). Eldest son of Gruffydd (died trying to escape from the Tower of London 1244), Llywelyn defeated the last of his brothers in 1255. By 1258 this grandson of Llywelyn ap Iorwerth became powerful enough to earn the style Prince of Wales, and received recognition from Henry III of England (1267). His Principality of Wales embraced Gwynedd, Powys, Deheubarth, and the March (lands bordering England). The English Barons' War enabled him to marry Simon de Montfort's daughter Eleanor (1278, died in childbirth 1282). Raids penetrated to

Llywelyn the Great on his deathbed watched by his sons Gruffydd and David 1240, from *The Greater Chronicle* of Matthew Paris

Dyfed, Gwent and Glamorgan. Soon, though, quarrels with his brother Dafydd weakened the allegiance of Llywelyn's Welsh vassals. He refused Edward I homage and in the war of 1276-7 lost control of all but west Gwynedd. His brother triggered another war with England and Llywelyn died in a skirmish at Builth. The last Prince of Wales was buried at his favoured Cistercian monastery of Cwn Hir and his only child Gwenllian died (1337) in an English Gilbertine nunnery at Sempringham, Lincolnshire.

(There followed a Welsh war of independence that collapsed in 1283. By then Edward I was already building garrisoned castles to enforce English control in Wales, and in 1287 English troops crushed a revolt by **Rhys ap Maredudd** *['son of Maredudd'], the last Prince of Deheubarth.*

In 1301 Edward I bestowed the honorary title Prince of Wales on his son, later Edward II. Since then no fewer than 20 first-born male heirs to the English, later British, throne have borne the title Prince of Wales.)

Owain Glyndwr (born c1355, died ? Monington, Herefordshire c1417). A descendant of the Powys princes as well as Lord of Glyndwr and Sycharth, in North Wales (with estates in Pembrokeshire) Glyndwr (Owen Glendower to the English) proclaimed himself Prince of Wales (1400). His epic revolt (1400-12) against Henry IV and English rule reached its peak in 1405 with control of

A Welsh prince sits
in judgement, 13th
century MS of the
Laws of Hywel Dda

Anglesey and most of the principality. France and
Scotland recognized the new Prince. The fall of
Harlech (1409) marked its effective end, but
Glyndwr was still leading a guerrilla band in 1412.
His daughter Alice married Sir Edmund Mortimer
(died 1409), greatest of the English Marcher lords.
Some sources relate that Glyndwr received a
pardon and enjoyed a peaceful retirement.

*(Owain Glyndwr's first cousin **Maredudd ap Tudur**
['son of Tudur'] , descended from the Llywelyn the
Great's youngest daughter, who joined his revolt
from Anglesey was the great-grandfather of the
Welsh prince **Henry Tudor** who in 1485 became
Henry VII of England. Henry's son **Henry VIII** in
1536 unified the government of England and
Wales.)*

High King Flann Sinna's Cross of the Scriptures at Clonmacnoise, Co Offaly. Flann (died 916) was also King of Meath and son of a high king

5. IRISH KINGS

More than a thousand kings and queens could have reigned in Ireland since prehistoric times.

Old Irish sagas show that in the early centuries AD Ireland was divided into about 150 tiny Celtic kingdoms with warrior kings elected from a landowning upper class whose main source of wealth was cattle. In time the kingdoms formed five groups each with one honorary overlord. From south to north these so-called Five Fifths were Munster (Mumha, 67 known kings including 3 High Kings, c450-1194); Leinster (Laighin, 68 known kings c436-1171); Meath (Midhe, 52 known kings including 8 High Kings, c450-1173); Connaught (Connacht, 64 known kings including 4 High Kings, c459-1224); and Ulster (Uladh, 72 known kings, c500-1201). Dominance could shift from one to another, and descendants of a king of Meath became High Kings of Ireland, ceremonially inaugurated on the hill of Tara, a mound-sanctuary on the River Boyne in Meath. But not all provincial kings acknowledged them as overlords.

Old Irish king lists name scores of provincial kings and 136 pre-Christian high kings (Christianity arrived in the 5th century AD). Foremost among them was the arguably historical figure of High King **Cormac mac Art** (reigned AD 227-266). Many early kings were probably legendary, but there emerged undoubted dynasties bearing such names as O'Brien (in Munster), O'Connor (in Connaught) and O'Neill (Meath). Founded by the semi-legendary **Niall of the Nine Hostages** (reigned

379-405) and continued by his son **Loeguire** (429-458) who reigned in the traditional year of St Patrick's mission to Ireland (432), the O'Neill dynasty based in Meath produced a long line of high kings. Between 734 and 1002 the high kingship alternated between northern and southern branches of the O'Neill family. Two of Niall's other sons founded the Kingdom of Aileach in 400 (area of the later city of Londonderry) which had 52 known sovereigns until 1170 including 18 High Kings. Other local monarchs such as Fergus of Dalriada (c500) crossed North Channel to seek wider domains (*see Kings and Queens of Scotland*).

From about 800 native Irish kings faced competition from foreigners. The first Viking invasion of Ireland (795) foreshadowed nearly two centuries when Norse kings ruled many tiny coastal states such as Dublin (838, 25 kings known for 856-1170), Waterford (914) and Limerick (920-68), although High King **Aed Finnliath** (reigned 862-879) drove them from Ulster. Powerful maritime rulers emerged, some using Ireland as a springboard for attacks on Scotland and England as well as trade with the Norse Kingdom of York (867-954) via the Clyde-Firth of Forth route. **Turgeis** (flourished about 839-845) seized northern Ireland and styled himself King of Dublin. **Olaf I** 'the White' united Ireland's Vikings in 853 and for 20 years styled himself 'King of the northmen of all Ireland and Britain'. **Ranald** (died 927) became King of Dublin, Waterford, and York. King **Olaf III Cuaran** of Dublin made a sea pilgrimage to

Iona in 980, beginning the Irish Norse change from
paganism to Christianity. Descendants of **Ranald**
of Waterford (reigned 1022-31) included Scotland's
Robert II, an ancestor of the present British royal
family.

Viking power in Ireland effectively ended in 1014
when **Brian Boru**, King of Munster from 976, and
High King of Ireland (born in Thomond, near
Killaloe, Co Clare 941; reigned 1002-1014) after
ousting **Mael Sechnaill II**, the last O'Neill occupant
of the Tara throne, assembled an army that won
the decisive Battle of Clontarf (23 April 1014) near
Dublin. Brian died in the fighting, but three
O'Brien descendants, beginning with his son
Donnchad (reigned 1014-1064) remained kings of
Munster until the next century (1119). The main
Munster kingship disappeared in 1194, but the
O'Briens remained kings of north Munster
(Thomond, later County Clare) until 1543. Their
kingdom then became a Henry VIII-created
earldom until 1741 when the 8th earl died childless.

After Brian Boru's death there followed 150
years of internal fighting between petty kings
claiming the high kingship of Ireland. This rivalry
indirectly finished Irish royal rule in Ireland. Its
downfall began in 1166 when the last High King
(56th known since Niall) **Rory O'Connor** (Ruaidri
Ua Conchobar), son of **Turlough** (Toirdelbach)
More O'Connor (born 1088; reigned 1119-1153),
expelled his rival **Dermot Macmurrough** (Diarmait
mac Murchad), last King of Leinster (born ?1110;
reigned 1134-1171). Dermot sought Anglo-Norman

help that led to an invasion begun in 1169. Its
leader Richard de Clare, 2nd Earl of Pembroke
(died 1176), known to history as Strongbow,
married Dermot's daughter Aoife (Eva). His
baronial army of about 1200 troops then captured
prosperous Wexford, Waterford and Dublin. In
1171 **Henry II** of England landed near Waterford to
assert crown rights, taking hostages, receiving
homage and ending the rule of the kings of Meath
(1173). In 1175 Rory O'Connor acknowledged
Henry as overlord, was deposed in 1186 and lived
until 1198. **Cathal O'Connor** succeeded as the last
King of Connaught in 1201, resisting English
advances until his death in 1224 as the last Irish
provincial monarch, but his native dynasty endured
until 1464.

At first, English rule of Ireland remained
nominal except around Dublin. Until Tudor times
and the creation of the Pale settlement, marcher
barons and Irish chiefs controlled the rest, and
English kings simply called themselves Lord of
Ireland. After Henry II, only John and Richard II
bothered to visit their westernmost island domain.
Then in 1541 **Henry VIII** styled himself King of
Ireland. Ireland remained under English and then
British kings and queens until Edward VIII's
abdication (1936). Apart from James II and
William III, George IV was the first monarch since
Richard II to visit Ireland. Then the new Irish Free
State abolished the monarchy in 1936 and formally
became a republic. British monarchs continued to

reign over Northern Ireland, comprising most of what had once been the ancient kingdom of Ulster.

The present British royal family can trace its ancestry back through two routes to Brian Boru. His ancient harp remains in the arms of Ireland.

Early Irish Kingdoms

6. SCOTTISH KINGS AND QUEENS

Forty-five legendary kings predate the Scottish (ie Irish) ruler said to have founded Scotland's first royal dynasty about AD 500. **Fergus**, son of Erc, ruled Dalriada, a Celtic kingdom once embracing part of Northern Ireland, the Inner Hebrides, and Argyll in Scotland. Fergus left Ireland and settled in Argyll. His Scots, under Fergus' 36 known named descendants during the next 343 years to **Kenneth MacAlpin**, shared what we now call Scotland with three other groups: the Picts of the north (see separate king list), the Britons of the south-west (Kingdom of Strathclyde, capital Dumbarton, see separate king list); and the Angles of the south-east. Later, Norse invaders seized parts of the far north and the Western Isles. Meanwhile, Dalriada's kings had begun uniting Scotland under Scottish rule.

Among the early Scots, a strong brother or cousin of the king rather than a male descendant inherited the throne. Later, sons tended to inherit from their fathers. Most early kings came from the line of Fergus; a few came from the line of Loarn (another son of Erc). Later intermarriage with England's royal family added Anglo-Norman blood.

From about AD 900 Scottish kings were inaugurated at Scone near Perth, like Pictish kings before them. Early Scottish and Pictish kings ruled from centres that included Dunkeld, Scone, and Abernethy. When they died, most early Scottish kings (including **Macbeth** and his stepson)were buried on the holy island of Iona in Dalriada.

Following the Strathclyde and Pictish king lists are brief details of all 42 Scottish sovereigns up to Mary. Queen of Scots. *(For James VI and later Scottish monarchs see Kings and Queens of Great Britain.)*

BRITISH KINGS OF STRATHCLYDE c450-1018 (PARTIAL LIST)

Ceretic (Coroticus) of Dumbarton c450

Rhydderch Hen died 603

Constantine son of (?) Rhydderch

(?)Iudruis died 633

Owain (Eugein) [defeated Scots] died 642

Gwraid (Gureit) died 658

Dyfnwal (Domhnall), son of Owain died 694

Beli, son of Elphin [twice defeated by Scots] died 722

Tewdwr (Teudubr), son of Beli died 750

Dyfnwal (Dannagual), son of Tewdwr died 760

Cynan, son of Ruadrach died 816

Artgha [Vikings sack Dumbarton 870] died 872

Run, son of Artgha died before (?) 878

Dyfnwal (Donevaldus) died 908

Dyfnwal (Donevaldus), son of Ede (Aedh) Owain [submitted to Edward the Elder of Wessex 925] died 934

Dyfnwal (Domhnall), son of Eoghain [probably defeated and killed Cuilean of Scotland 971] died on pilgrimage 975

Malcolm, son of Dyfnwal [homage to Edgar of
   England] died 997
Owain (Eugenius) the Bald [allied to Malcolm II of
   Scotland at Battle of Carham 1018]

KINGS OF THE PICTS c556-848

Bridei I [visited by St Columba] c556-c586
Gartnart, son of Bridei I's sister c586-597
Nectu, son of Gartnart's sister
Cinioch, son of Gartnat's sister died 631
Garnard, son of Cinioch's sister 631-635
Bridei II, brother of Garnard 635-641
Talorc, brother of Garnard 641-653
Talorcen (Tolargan), son of Eanfrith of Bernicia
   653-657
Gartnait, son of Talorcen's sister 657-663
Drest I, brother of Gartnait 663-671
Bridei III, son of Drest I's sister [victor of
   Nechtanesmere 685] 671-692
Taran, son of Bridei III's sister 692-696
Bridei IV, son of Drest I's sister 696-706
Nechton, brother of Bridei IV [adopted Roman
   Catholicism 710] 706-724
Drest II, son of Nechton's sister 724-726
Alpin I, brother of Nechton 726-728
Onuist, son of Taran's sister 728-761
Bridei V, brother of Onuist 761-763
Ciniod, son of Onuist's sister 763-775
Alpin II, son of Ciniod's sister 775-780
Drest III, son of Alpin II's sister 780-781
Talorcan, son of Alpin II's sister 781-785

Talorgen I, son of Onuist 785-787
Canaul, son of Alpin II's sister 787-789
Constantine, son of Alpin II's sister 789-820
Unuist, brother of Drest IV 820-834
Drest IV, son of Uen 834-837
Uen (Eoganan of Dalriada), son of Unuist 837-839
Uurad 839-842
Bred, son of Uurad 842
Kineth, son of Uurad 842
Brude, son of Uurad's sister 843-845
Drust, son of Uurad 845-848

The House of Fergus and Loarn 843-1058

Scotland's first ruling dynasty descended from the line of Dalriada (Argyll) kings founded by Fergus about AD 500. These monarchs had intermarried with the Picts. The Loarn strand stemmed from Fergus' brother and included Macbeth and his stepson Lulach.

Kenneth I MacAlpin (died 858), son of Alpin (died c837) who was son of King of the Scots (Dalriada) Eochaid IV the Venomous and a Pictish heiress. King of the Scots (from 841), Kenneth subdued the Picts and became the first King of the Picts and

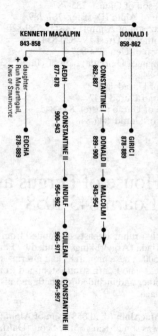

THE HOUSES OF FERGUS AND LOARN 843-1058 (continued next page)

KENNETH MACALPIN
843-858

DONALD I
858-862

daughter
+ Run Macarthgail,
King of Strathclyde

AEDH
877-878

CONSTANTINE I
862-887

GIRIC I
878-889

EOCHA
878-889

CONSTANTINE II
900-943

DONALD II
899-900

INDULF
954-962

MALCOLM I
943-954

CUILEAN
966-971

CONSTANTINE III
995-997

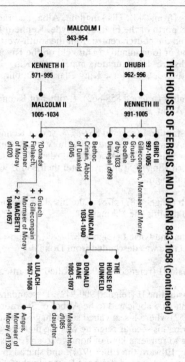

THE HOUSES OF FERGUS AND LOARN 843-1058 (continued)

MALCOLM I
943-954

KENNETH II
971-995

DHUBH
962-996

MALCOLM II
1005-1034

KENNETH III
991-1005

+ ?Donada
Mormaer
of Moray
d1020

Bethoc
+ Crinan, Abbot
of Dunkeld
d1045

GIRIC II
997-1005
Gillecomgain, Mormaer of Moray
+ Gruach
Boedhe
d by 1033
Dunegal d599

+ Gruach
+ 1 Gillecomgain
Mormaer of Moray
+ 2 **MACBETH**
1040-1057

DUNCAN I
1034-1040

**THE
HOUSE OF
DUNKELD**

LULACH
1057-1058

**DONALD
BANE**
1093-1097

Maelsnechtai
d1085

daughter

Angus,
Mormaer of
Moray d1130

Scots (from 843). His kingdom, Alba, embraced lands north of the Firth and Clyde. Kenneth I moved the church centre from the south-westerly island of Iona inland to Dunkeld on the River Tay, Perthshire. His daughters married the King of Strathclyde and Norse King Olaf I of Dublin.

Donald I (reigned 858-862). Brother of Kenneth MacAlpin.

Constantine I (reigned 862-877), son of Kenneth MacAlpin, killed in battle by the Vikings, but his sister married Run Macarthgail (died 872) the British King of Strathclyde and their son Eocha would reign.

Aedh (reigned 877-878). Like his elder brother died fighting the Vikings.

Eocha and **Giric I** (reigned 878-889). Deposed in 889. Giric was descended from Donald I.

Donald II (reigned 889-900). Killed in battle.

Constantine II (reigned 900-942). Descendant of Aedh who abdicated to be Abbot of St Andrews (d 952) where his so-called sarcophagus remains. During his secular reign he was the first Scottish king to render a kind of homage to an English king, Edward the Elder (924), and shared in the great northerners' defeat at Brunanburh (937),

losing a son, at the hands of Edward's son
Athelstan.

Malcolm I (reigned 943-954). Another reign ended
by death in battle.

Indulf (reigned 954-962). Abdicated.

Dhubh (Duff) (reigned 962-966). Killed in battle.

Cuilean (reigned 966-971). Killed.

Kenneth II (reigned 971-995). Murdered brother of
Dhubh, he obtained Lothian from the English
King Edgar the Peaceable.

Constantine III (reigned 995-997). Murdered.

Kenneth III (reigned 997-1005). Killed in battle by
Malcolm II. **Giric II** was his son and co-ruler.

Malcolm II (born c954; reigned 1016 to 25 Nov
1034, died at Glamis). Son of Kenneth II and King
of Alba (1005-34), Malcolm effectively became the
first king of Scotland about 1016 when he made his
grandson Duncan king of the old British kingdom
of Strathclyde. He next defeated the
Northumbrians at Carham on the Tweed (1018).
Malcolm then controlled lands extending beyond
the old Alba to take in the English-speaking
Angles of south-east Scotland, and Welsh-speaking
Britons in the south-west. His daughter married

Sigurd II the Stout, the 13th-known Norse Earl of Orkney (the first Earl or Jarl ruled from c874). Malcolm was probably a pious Christian and had his headquarters in Fife, perhaps at Dunkeld.

Duncan I (born c1010; reigned 1034 to 1 Aug 1040). Through his mother Bethoc he was the grandson of Malcolm II who chose him as his successor. Duncan's father was Cronan (Crinan), Abbot of Dunkeld, hence his dynasty's name: House of Dunkeld. Near Elgin Duncan I died fighting a rival claimant to the throne, Macbeth.

Macbeth (born c1005; reigned 1040 to 15 Aug 1057). He became one of three kings dominating 11th-century Scotland. A member of the junior royal line (of Loarn), and mormaer (ruler) of the province of Moray, Macbeth was married to Kenneth III's grand-daughter Gruach. He became king of Scotland by killing his cousin Duncan I (1040) of the line of Fergus, and driving out Duncan's elder sons Malcolm and Donald Bane. During his reign Macbeth probably made a pilgrimage to Rome. Intervention by Edward the Confessor of England, who sent Earl Siward of Northumbria in favour of Malcolm, brought Macbeth's defeat at Dunsinane Hill near Scone (1054). He fled north but was killed by Malcolm at Lumphanan.

Lulach (born c1032; reigned 15 Aug 1057 to 17 Mar 1058). Macbeth's stepson became King of Scots after Macbeth's death but was soon killed in an ambush. Nevertheless he left Celtic descendants who disputed the throne for another century.

The House of Dunkeld 1058-1371

Macbeth's overthrower Malcolm III began a dynasty that lasted three centuries. Although its direct line died out in 1290, Robert the Bruce triumphantly reasserted Scotland's monarchy in the teeth of England's claims during the Scottish War of Independence (1296-1328).

Malcolm III 'Canmore' (born c1031; reigned 17 Mar 1058 to 13 Nov 1093; died near Alnwick, Northumberland). His reign began more than two centuries' almost unbroken rule by the House of Dunkeld (alias Canmore, or 'chief'). Exiled to England during the reign of Macbeth, with English military help he defeated (1054) and killed (1057) Macbeth, and became King of all Scotland (crowned 25 Apr 1058) after the death of Macbeth's stepson and successor Lulach. Malcolm's first marriage, to Ingibjorg, widow of Earl Thorfinn II of Orkney, strengthened ties with

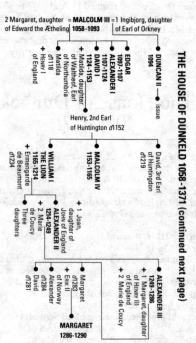

THE HOUSE OF DUNKELD 1058-1371 (continued next page)

2 Margaret, daughter = **MALCOLM III** = 1 Ingibjorg, daughter
of Edward the Ætheling **1058-1093** of Earl of Orkney

Matilda
d1118
+ Henry I
of England

DAVID I
1124-1153
+ Matilda, daughter
of Waltheof, Earl
of Northumbria

ALEXANDER I
1107-1124

EDGAR
1097-1107

DUNCAN II
1094 ● — issue

Henry, 2nd Earl
of Huntington d1152

WILLIAM I
THE LION
1165-1214
+ Ermengarde
de Beaumont
d1234

MALCOLM IV
1153-1165

David, 3rd Earl
of Huntington
d1219

Three
daughters

ALEXANDER II
1214-1249
+ 1 Joan,
daughter of John
of England
+ 2 Marie
de Coucy

ALEXANDER III
1249-1286
+ 1 Margaret, daughter
of Henry III
of England
+ 2 Marie de Coucy

David
d1281

Alexander
d1284
+ Erik II
of Norway

Margaret
d1263

MARGARET
1286-1290

THE HOUSE OF DUNKELD 1058-1371 (continued)

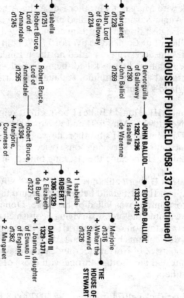

David, 3rd Earl of Huntingdon d1219

Isabella
d1251
+ Robert Bruce,
Lord of
Annandale
d1245

Margaret
d1228
+ Alan, Lord
of Galloway
d234

Robert Bruce,
Lord of
Annandale
d295

Devorguilla
of Galloway
d290
+ John Balliol
d269

JOHN BALLIOL
1292-1296
+ Isabella
de Warenne

'EDWARD BALLIOL'
1332-1341

Robert Bruce,
Earl of
Annandale
d304
+ Marjorie,
Countess of
Carrick

ROBERT I
1306-1329
+ 1 Isabella
of Mar
d316
+ 2 Elizabeth
de Burgh
d327

Marjorie
d316
+ Walter the
Steward
d326

THE
HOUSE OF
STEWART

DAVID II
1329-1371
+ 1 Joanna, daughter
of Edward II
of England
d362
+ 2 Margaret
Drummond
d375

the Scandinavians of north Scotland. His second
(c1070), to Margaret (St Margaret c1045-93),
introduced English influences and forged a royal
link with Margaret's brother Edgar the Atheling,
an Anglo-Saxon prince (died c1125) with a claim on
the English throne. Malcolm acknowledged
William I of England as overlord (1072) but five
times unsuccessfully invaded northern England.
The fifth time he was killed, being buried with
Margaret at Dunfermline. A daughter married
England's Henry I.

Donald III (Donald Bane) (born c1031; reigned
13 Nov 1093 to May 1094 and 12 Nov 1094 to Oct
1097). Malcolm III's brother, he was opposed by
Malcolm's two surviving sons, twice deposed, and
blinded. He became the last king buried on Iona.

Duncan II (born c1060; reigned May-12 Nov 1094).
William II of England helped him secure the
throne but he was killed by his uncle, Donald III.
He granted the oldest surviving Scottish charter.
He was the son of Malcolm III and Ingibjorg and
his descendants by Ethelreda, daughter of Earl
Gospatrick of Northumberland, unsuccessfully
contested the Scottish throne with those of his half-
brothers.

Edgar (born c1074; reigned Oct 1097 to c8 Jan
1107). Son of Malcolm III and Margaret. He
acknowledged England's William II as overlord
and in 1098 ceded the Hebrides to Norway's

Magnus III. Edgar was a church benefactor. He did not marry.

Alexander I the Fierce (born c1080; reigned c8 Jan 1107 to Apr 1124). He succeeded his brother Edgar but let the youngest brother David rule southern Scotland (Cumbria, Strathclyde and South Lothian).Alexander married Sibylla, natural daughter of England's Henry I, and participated in Henry's 1114 Welsh campaign.

David I the Saint (born c1084; reigned Apr 1124 to 24 May 1153, died Carlisle, Cumberland). This influential king established a basic form of central government; issued the first royal coinage; built the castle nuclei of Berwick, Edinburgh, and Stirling; and strengthened Anglo-Norman aristocratic and feudal influence in Scotland. This followed his early years at the court of England's Henry I, David's brother-in-law, where he was 1st Earl of Huntingdon. From 1136 David fought for his niece Matilda against Stephen in the English civil wars, and secured parts of Cumberland and Northumberland for himself. He modified Scottish Christianity (5 bishoprics founded) and established great Lowland abbeys on mainstream West European monastic lines.

Malcolm IV the Maiden (born 1141; reigned 24 May 1153 to 9 Dec 1165, died Jedburgh Abbey, Roxburghshire). Son of Henry, Earl of Northumberland, he was only about 12 when he

David I and his grandson Malcolm IV from a 1159 charter to Kelso Abbey

succeeded his grandfather David I whose English conquests he yielded to Henry II in return for resuming the Earldom of Huntingdon. Malcolm did manage to subdue the Galloway Celts and Somerled, Lord of the Isles and founder of the Macdonald clan. He was perhaps the last Gaelic-speaking monarch and did not marry although he left a natural son.

William I the Lion (born c1143; reigned 9 Dec 1165 to 4 Dec 1214, died Stirling). Younger brother of

Malcolm IV, William fought to regain
Northumberland from England, beginning the
'Auld Alliance' with France, but was captured at
Alnwick and forced to acknowledge Henry II as
Scotland's overlord (1174). He bought back
Scotland's sovereignty from Richard I for £6600
(1189) towards the Third Crusade and in 1192 won
long-canvassed papal recognition of the Scottish
Church's independence under Rome. William
strengthened central authority, notably in
Caithness, issued charters for a number of
important burghs, and probably introduced the
lion rampant to Scotland's royal arms. He married
Ermengarde de Beaumont and was buried at his
rich 1178 foundation, Arbroath Abbey.

Alexander II (born Haddington, E Lothian 24 Aug
1198; reigned 4 Dec 1214 to 8 July 1249, died
Kerrera Island, Argyll). Red-haired son of William
'the Lion', he stamped his rule on dissident Argyll
(1222), Caithness (from 1222), Galloway (from
1235) and Moray, but fought fruitlessly to regain
northern counties of England. He agreed with
Henry III the Peace of York (1237), which put the
Anglo-Scottish boundary roughly where it is now,
and was granted English northern estates worth
£200 a year. He married (1) Joan (died 1238),
eldest legitimate daughter of King John of
England, 1221 and (2) Marie de Coucy of Picardy,
daughter of Baron Enguerrand de Coucy and
mother of Alexander III.
Alexander II is buried at Melrose Abbey.

Great Seal of
Alexander III

Alexander III (born 4 Sept 1241; reigned 8 July 1249 to 19 Mar 1286, died near Kinghorn, Fife). After a long minority until 1262 during which he was seized by rival court factions, he defeated a Norwegian invasion and bought the Isle of Man and the Hebrides for £2666 from Norway's Magnus VI (1266). Alexander kept on good terms with England, attending Edward I's coronation, but refused to do homage. He married (1) Henry III's daughter Margaret (1240-75) at York 1251 and (2) the Comte de Dreux's daughter Yolande (1285). He outlived his two sons and a daughter, being killed when his horse jumped off a cliff during a night ride.

Margaret 'the Maid of Norway' (born cApr 1283; reigned 19 Mar 1286 to c26 Sept 1290, died in the Orkneys). Last of the line of Malcolm III, she was a grand-daughter of Alexander III, his acknowledged heir from 1284, and daughter of

King Erik II of Norway (r1280-99). She died on a voyage from Norway (and was buried in Bergen) pledged to marry the future Edward II of England. Edward I then declared himself Scotland's overlord. There followed an interregnum (1290-2) and three decades of fighting.

John Balliol (born c1250, died Normandy Apr 1313; reigned 17 Nov 1292 to 10 July 1296). Of Norman ancestry, this grandson of David I's eldest daughter was chosen king by England's Edward I from among 13 competitors. When the Scots rejected Edward as overlord and Balliol signed an alliance with France, Edward invaded Scotland, won the Battle of Dunbar (1296), forced Balliol to abdicate, and seized the coronation stone of Scone. A second Scottish royal interregnum followed (1296-1306). Balliol married Isabella, daughter of John de la Warenne, 6th Earl of Surrey, and had two sons.

Robert I (born Writtle, near Chelmsford, Essex 11 July 1274; reigned 27 Mar 1306 to 7 June 1329, died Cardross Castle on the Clyde, Dumbartonshire). He became a national hero for winning Scotland's independence from England, although a supporter of Edward I until 1298 and in 1302-5. Robert de Bruce VIII, 2nd Earl of Carrick, was a leading member of an Anglo-Norman family and a great grandson of David I via that king's second daughter's marriage. Robert seized the vacant Scottish throne in 1306 after stabbing to death his

Great Seal of Robert I

rival John Comyn the Red, Balliol's nephew, at
Dumfries. Edward I's troops drove him into
hiding, but after Edward's death guerrilla tactics
(the spider's web story dates from the 16th century)

gradually gained the upper hand. Robert won the decisive Battle of Bannockburn (1314) against Edward II in person. He and his younger brother **Edward** (crowned King of Ireland, but killed at the Battle of Dundalk, 5 Oct 1318) invaded Ulster and northern England (Berwick captured 1318), forcing the young Edward III to abandon his claims on Scotland by the Treaty of Northampton (1328).

Robert married (1) Isabella, daughter of Donald, 6th Earl of Mar, 1295, by whom he had a daughter Marjorie (died 1316), and (2) Elizabeth (died 1327), daughter of Richard de Burgh, 3rd Earl of Ulster, 1302 by whom he had two sons and two daughters. Bruce possibly died of leprosy and is buried at Dunfermline (his heart at Melrose Abbey).

David II (born Dunfermline 5 Mar 1324; reigned with interruptions 7 June 1329 to 22 Feb 1371, died Edinburgh Castle). He was the only surviving son of Robert I, but, after becoming Scotland's first annointed monarch (Scone, 24 Nov 1331), he was forced into French exile (1334) by John Balliol's pro-English son Edward Balliol. David returned in June 1341. Invading England, he was defeated, wounded and captured at Neville's Cross, Durham (17 Oct 1346) remaining imprisoned until the Treaty of Berwick (1357). Instead of completing £66,000 ransom payments he offered (1363-4) to make an English prince his heir. He married (1) (while aged four) Edward III's sister Joanna (1321-62) 17 July 1328, and (2) Margaret Drummond

David II (left) shakes hands with Edward III of England
1357

(died 1375), widow of Sir John Logie, Dec 1363 (divorced Mar 1370).David II died childless and is buried at Holyroodhouse.

Edward Balliol ('reigned' 24 Sept 1332 to 1341; died Wheatley, S Yorks Jan 1364). Eldest son of John Balliol, he was Edward III's claimant to the throne. The younger Balliol and other disinherited lords invaded from France, defeating and killing David II's Regent, Donald, 7th Earl of Mar, at Dupplin Moor (12 Aug 1332). Balliol was crowned Edward I at Scone only to be defeated at Annan (Dumfries) by another Scots army on 16 Dec. Edward III then intervened and defeated the victorious Sir Archibald Douglas at Halidon Hill (19 July 1333). In return Balliol ceded England much of the Lowlands, but effectively lost the realm after 1341 while the Anglo-French-Scottish struggle continued. Balliol gave up his claims and all his lands to Edward III on 21 Jan 1356.

The House of Stewart 1371-1567

The dynasty that would ultimately rule England as well as Scotland started with Robert II, son of Robert the Bruce's daughter Marjorie and her husband Walter the Steward. After Robert III's

THE HOUSE OF STEWART 1371-1567 (continued next page)

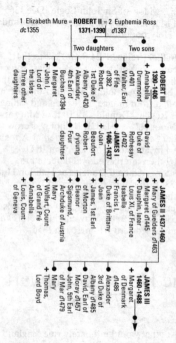

1 Elizabeth Mure = **ROBERT II** = 2 Euphemia Ross
dc1355   **1371-1390**   d1387

Two daughters   Two sons

ROBERT III
1390-1406
+ Annabella Drummond d1401

Robert, 1st Duke of Albany d1420

Alexander, 4th Earl of Buchan d1394

Margaret + John I, Lord of the Isles

Three other daughters

Walter, Earl of Fife d1362

David, Duke of Rothesay d1402

JAMES I
1406-1437
+ Joan Beaufort

Robert d young

Four daughters

Isabella + Francis I, Duke of Brittany

Margaret + Louis XI, of France

JAMES II 1437-1460
+ Mary of Guelders d1463

Louis, Count of Geneva

Annabella + Louis, Count of Grand Pré

Margaret + Wolfart, Count of Grand Pré

Mary + Wolfart, Count of Grand Pré

Eleanor + Sigismund, Archduke of Austria

Joan + James, 1st Earl of Morton

JAMES III
1460-1488
+ Margaret of Denmark d1486

Alexander 3rd Duke of Albany d1485

David, Earl of Moray d1457

John, 5th Earl of Mar d1479

Mary + Thomas, Lord Boyd

(continued next page)

THE HOUSE OF STEWART 1371-1567 (continued)

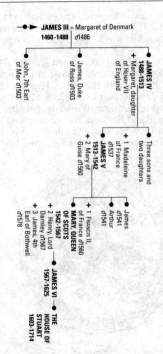

JAMES III = Margaret of Denmark
1460-1488 d1486

John, 7th Earl of Mar d1503

James, Duke of Ross d1503

JAMES IV = Margaret, daughter of Henry VII of England
1488-1513

Three sons and two daughters

James d1541

Arthur d1541

JAMES V + 1 Madeleine of France d1537
1513-1542 + 2 Mary of Guise d1560

MARY, QUEEN OF SCOTS + 1 Francis II, of France d1560
1542-1567 + 2 Henry, Lord Darnley d1567
+ 3 James, 4th Earl of Bothwell d1578

JAMES VI — THE HOUSE OF STUART
1567-1625 1603-1714

death in 1406, five successive Jameses reigned in
Scotland until 1542. James V's only surviving and
eleventh-hour child was Mary, Queen of Scots.

Robert II (born 2 Mar 1316; reigned 22 Feb 1371 to
19 Apr 1390, died Dundonald, Ayrshire). Son of
Walter the Steward (6th Hereditary High Steward
of Scotland), and Robert I's daughter Marjorie, he
founded the Stewart (Stuart) dynasty that later
ruled Scotland and England. Before accession he
had been successively joint and sole regent in
David II's absence. During his reign, from 1384,

Great Seal of Robert II

his two sons were the real rulers for their unmilitary father. He married (1) Elizabeth Mure (a relative), daughter of Sir Adam Mure, c1348 after she bore nine children; and (2) Euphemia Ross (died 1387), widowed Countess of Moray and daughter of Hugh, Earl of Ross, having two sons and two daughters. Robert the Steward also had a minimum of eight illegitimate children. The later nickname King Blearie referred to his bloodshot eyes.

Robert III (born c1337; reigned 19 Apr 1390 to 4 Apr 1406, died Rothesay, Bute). Eldest son of Robert II and Elizabeth Mure and known as John Stewart, Earl of Carrick, before accession, his active kingship was crippled by the kick of a horse. Highlanders descended on the Lowlands and power was disputed between his brother Robert, Earl of Fife and 1st Duke of Albany (Scotland's first duke from 1398), and the King's eldest son David, 1st Duke of Rothesay (murdered at Falkland 1402). Robert III married Annabella (died 1401), daughter of Sir John Drummond, by whom he had three sons and four daughters.

James I (born Dunfermline Dec 1394; reigned 4 Apr 1406 to 21 Feb 1437). Robert III's second son, he was caught by the English sailing to France in 1406 and held mainly in the Tower of London until 1424. The Governor in his absence was his uncle Robert, 1st Duke of Albany (died 1420) and the latter's son. His belated rule, after a £40,000 ransom, proved severe and unpopular and he was murdered in the Monastery of the Preaching Friars at Perth by Sir Robert Graham in a family dispute over the throne.

He married Joan (c1400-45), daughter of John Beaufort, 1st Duke of Somerset, 2 Feb 1424 in London. They had twin sons and seven daughters. James I is buried at Perth in his Carthusian monastic foundation. During captivity he wrote the famous poem *Kingis Quair* ('the King's Book').

James II (born Holyrood Monastery, Edinburgh 16 Oct 1430; reigned 21 Feb 1437 to 3 Aug 1460). He was the surviving twin son of James I and a large birthmark bequeathed the nickname Fiery Face. His coronation at Kelso Abbey was the first not at Scone. By giving authority to men of his own choice, and travelling energetically, James II strengthened a monarchy weakened by powerful nobles. In particular he murdered the 8th and killed the 9th Earl of Douglas (1452-5). He married Mary of Guelders (died 1463), daughter of Arnold, Duke of Guelders (a Rhine principality) 3 July 1449 at Holyrood. They had four sons and two daughters. James was killed by an exploding cannon as he besieged English-held Roxburgh which his queen then took.

James III (born May 1452; reigned 3 Aug 1460 to 11 June 1488). Eldest son of James II, he failed, after a minority ending in 1469, to assert his own authority against two noblemen's rebellions backed by his own son, the later James IV. The artistic and homosexually-inclined James was caught and murdered by a soldier impersonating a priest after losing the Battle of Sauchieburn (near Bannockburn, Stirling) and being wounded. His wife Margaret (c1457-86) was the daughter of King Christian I of Denmark and Norway, the dowry being the Orkneys, Shetlands and Western Isles. They married at Holyroodhouse 13 July 1469 and had three sons.

James IV (born 17 Mar 1473; reigned 11 June 1488 to 9 Sept 1513, died near Branxton, Northumberland).The first king for a century fit to rule from the outset, James strengthened royal authority, brought all Scotland unity (last Lord of the Isles, John II, suppressed 1493), and, multi-lingual himself, gave her international status. A Renaissance prince, James was a wide-ranging patron and built a modern navy. He sporadically fought England in support of the Yorkist pretender Perkin Warbeck (1495-7). His 8 Aug 1503 marriage at Holyroodhouse to Henry VII's eldest daughter Margaret Tudor (1489-1541), by whom he had four sons and two daughters, became a basis for Stuart rule in England.

Siding with France in 1513, James invaded England, in the face of papal excommunication and advisers' pleas for caution, and died fighting on foot in the disastrous Battle of Flodden; the last king in Britain to fall in battle. His 20-year-old illegitimate son Alexander, Chancellor of Scotland, was among the realm's annihilated leadership. James's supposed body lies in the Church of St Michael, Wood Street, City of London.

James V (born Linlithgow 10 Apr 1512; reigned 9 Sept 1513 to 14 Dec 1542, died Falkland, Fife). Succeeding his father aged 17 months, the Poor Man's King became a puppet between pro-English Protestant and pro-French Catholic factions. James was imprisoned (1526-8) by his mother's second husband, Archibald, the pro-English 6th Earl of Angus, but escaped and asserted his authority as a pro-French Roman Catholic king.

His alliance with France and refusal to meet Henry VIII at York provoked an English response that routed the invading Scots at Solway Moss (24 Nov 1542). Already ill, the King broke down and died. James's wives were (1) Madeleine de Valois (1520-37), daughter of King Francis I of France, at Notre Dame, France 1 Jan 1537; and (2) Mary of Guise (1515-60), daughter of Claude, 1st Duke of Guise and Duke of Lorraine, and mother of Mary, Queen of Scots, 1538 by proxy in Paris and at St Andrews in June. Two infant sons died in 1541 and a daughter was born only a week before James died.

Mary, Queen of Scots (born Linlithgow 7 Dec 1542; reigned 14 Dec 1542 to 24 July 1567, died Fotheringhay Castle, Northants 8 Feb 1587). Mary's life was haunted by plots and murders and ended with her execution.

Contemporary drawing of Darnley's strangled body
1567

Mary's trial at Fotheringhay Castle 15 Oct 1586

She became Scotland's queen when only seven days old and was crowned in Stirling. After a Roman Catholic childhood in France she married the Dauphin Francis (24 Apr 1558), later Francis II (died 5 Dec 1560). On his death she returned to Scotland (1561) and married her 19-year-old first cousin Henry Stewart (Stuart), Lord Darnley, son of the 4th Earl of Lennox, on 29 July 1565 at Holyroodhouse Chapel. Their son was the future James VI (James I of England). Mary became estranged from Darnley (created Duke of Albany and styled Henry King of Scots) after he schemed the murder of her personal secretary David Rizzio. Then Darnley was strangled (10 Feb 1567) at Kirk o' Field, Edinburgh, probably by James, 4th Earl of Bothwell, who divorced his wife and became Mary's next (Protestant) husband (15 May 1567) at Holyroodhouse Chapel. Outraged Scottish Lords Associators then imprisoned the Queen and forced her abdication in favour of her baby son. She escaped to England, where she was heir to the throne. Fearing pro-Catholic plots to make Mary Queen of England, her cousin Elizabeth I imprisoned Mary and eventually had her executed. She was buried at Peterborough Cathedral until transferred in 1612 by her son to Henry VII's Chapel, Westminster Abbey.

(For subsequent Kings of Scotland see Kings and Queens of Great Britain.)

The first two Williams above Henry I and Stephen. All hold a church foundation

The Houses of Normandy and Blois 1066-1135

William II, 7th Duke of Normandy, founded this dynasty by killing Harold II to become William I of England. Norman rule introduced Norman French language, architecture, feudalism, and administration, based on castles. Matilda, the last (uncrowned) Norman sovereign, and the only female one, unsuccessfully fought Stephen, a rival claimant and England's only ruler of the House of Blois.

WILLIAM I 1066-1087
Nicknames The Bastard, later the Conqueror
Authority King of England and Duke of Normandy
Dynasty House of Normandy
Parents Robert I the Devil, 6th Duke of Normandy and Herleva (Arlette) of Conteville
Born Falaise Castle 1027 or 1028
Succeeded to throne 14 Oct 1066
Crowned Westminster Abbey 25 Dec 1066
Reigned 20 years, 330 days
Died Priory of St Gervais, near Rouen 9 Sept 1087
Buried St Stephen's Abbey, Caen
Married Matilda of Flanders (died 1083) 1052/1 at Eu Cathedral, Normandy
Children Nine, notably Robert (c1053-1134), William II, Henry I, and Adela (c1034-1137)

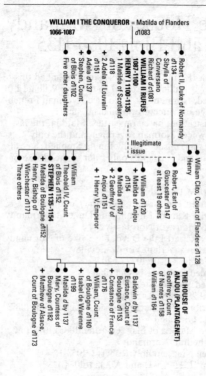

THE HOUSES OF NORMANDY AND BLOIS 1066-1135

WILLIAM I THE CONQUEROR = Matilda of Flanders
1066-1087   d1083

+ Robert II, Duke of Normandy
  d134
+ Sibylla of
  Conversano
+ Richard d c1081
+ **WILLIAM II RUFUS**
  1087-1100
+ **HENRY I 1100-1135**
+ 1 Matilda of Scotland
  d1118
+ 2 Adela of Louvain
  d151
+ Adela d137
+ Stephen, Count
  of Blois d1102
  Five other daughters

William Clito, Count of Flanders d1128
Henry

Robert, Earl of
Gloucester d1147
at least 19 others

William d120
+ Matilda of Anjou
  d154
+ Matilda d167
+ 2 Geoffrey V of
  Anjou d151
+ 1 Henry V, Emperor

Illegitimate
issue

**THE HOUSE OF
ANJOU (PLANTAGENET)**
Geoffrey, Count
of Names d158
William d164

William
Theobald IV, Count
of Blois d1152
+ Matilda of Boulogne d152
STEPHEN 1135-1154
Henry, Bishop of
Winchester d1171
Three others

Baldwin d by 1137
Eustace, Count of
Boulogne d1153
+ Constance of France
William, Count
of Boulogne d1160
+ Isabel de Warenne
d199
Mary, Countess of
Boulogne d182
Matilda d by 1137
+ Matthew of Alsace,
Count of Boulogne d173

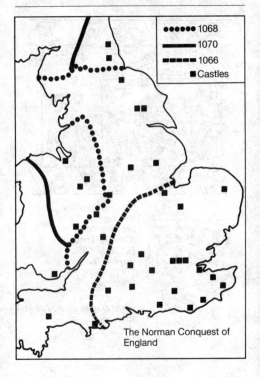

The Norman Conquest of England

Legend	
••••••	1068
——	1070
– – –	1066
■	Castles

ODO:EPS: ROTBERT:·ISTE·IVSS

WIL LELM:

William I consults
with his half-
brothers Odo
(c1030-97) and
Robert (d1091),
Bayeux Tapestry

Royal coat of arms, William I
to Henry I

William I receives *The Deeds of the Norman Dukes* from their chronicler William of Jumièges, early 12th century MS

Key facts England's first Norman king by right of conquest.

The illegitimate son of a Norman duke and his mistress, William inherited Normandy in 1035 and crushed revolts with help from the French king. Uneducated but shrewd and forceful, he pursued two main claims on the throne of England: first, his childless uncle Edward the Confessor had allegedly named William his heir; second, Edward's brother-in-law Harold had promised to back William's claim, when shipwrecked and imprisoned by William in 1064.

When Harold himself became king, William accordingly invaded England to overthrow him. William landed a Norman-French army on 28 September 1066. On 14 October his troops killed

Harold and defeated his Anglo-Saxon army at the Battle of Hastings. Crowned king on Christmas Day, William ruthlessly put down local revolts and gave conquered lands (78 castles recorded as built) to his followers in return for military service. He invaded Scotland (1072) and Wales (1081) to make England's borders secure. William let the English keep their own courts and laws, levied a land tax, and published a great land survey known as the *Domesday Book* (1086).

William died in France of an abdominal injury, due to a fall from horseback at the sack of Mantes. He left Normandy and Maine to his eldest son Robert and England to his second son William.

WILLIAM II 1087-1100
Nickname Rufus ('the red', from his florid complexion)
Authority King of England, with powers over Scotland, Wales, and Normandy
Dynasty House of Normandy
Parents William I and Matilda of Flanders, their third son
Born Normandy about 1056
Succeeded to throne 10 Sept 1087
Crowned Westminster Abbey 26 Sept 1087
Reigned 12 years, 326 days
Died near Lyndhurst, New Forest 2 Aug 1100
Buried Winchester Cathedral
Unmarried
Children None legitimate

WILLELMO·SECVN

William II on a Westminster Abbey column capital

Key facts William II Rufus subdued Scotland and Wales and gained control over Normandy. His most enduring monument is St Stephen's Hall, Westminster.

Rufus inherited England but his elder brother Robert Curthose inherited Normandy. The King smashed pro-Robert revolts by Norman barons in England (1088, 1095). He also invaded Scotland, later killing King Malcolm III (1093), and making Malcolm's successors his vassals. Cumberland and

Westmoreland were first annexed to the English crown.

Rufus subdued Wales (1097) and built castles there, but seizing Normandy from the incompetent Robert was his chief aim. Rufus invaded the Duchy (1091, 1094) and undermined Robert's power. In 1096 Robert mortgaged Normandy to his brother in return for cash to help pay for Robert's part in the First Crusade.

Rufus died hunting in the New Forest. He was shot in the back by an arrow probably fired by a supporter of his younger brother Henry; Henry then seized the throne.

HENRY I 1100-1135
Nicknames Beauclerk (unusually good reader), Lion of Justice
Authority King of England and (from 1106) Duke of Normandy
Dynasty House of Normandy
Parents William I and Matilda of Flanders, their fourth son
Born Selby, Yorkshire late 1068
Succeeded to throne 2 Aug 1100
Crowned Westminster Abbey 5 Aug 1100
Reigned 35 years, 122 days

Right: Henry I dreams of revolting peasants, rebellious nobles and clamouring prelates, from John of Worcester's *Chronicle* c1140

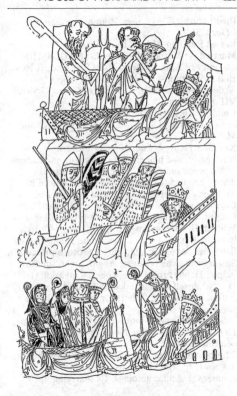

Died Lyons-la-Forêt, near Rouen, Normandy
1 Dec 1135
Buried Reading Abbey, Berkshire
Married (1) Matilda (formerly Edith) (1080-1118),
daughter of King Malcolm III of Scotland, 11 Nov
1100 at Westminster Abbey and (2) Adela
(Adelaide)(died 1151), daughter of Count Godfrey
VII of Louvain, 29 Jan 1121
Children Three by (1), notably William (b1103,
drowned in the 1120 'White Ship' shipwreck) and
Matilda
Key facts Henry bolstered royal authority, gained
Normandy, and helped unite Normans and Saxons.

Crowned only three days after William II's
death, he quickly consolidated power before he
could be challenged by his eldest brother Robert
Curthose of Normandy (returning from the First
Crusade). A Charter of Liberties promised to end
William II's unpopular taxes, seizures of Church
lands, and other legal abuses; while Henry pleased
Scots and Saxons by marrying a Scottish princess of
Saxon birth. The resulting Anglo-Saxon support
helped Henry brush aside Robert's invasion (1101).
Henry himself then invaded and seized Normandy
(1106), imprisoning Robert for life in Cardiff
Castle.

Securing his goals more by diplomacy than war,
Henry strengthened the Norman system of
centralized government and justice, and won Church
agreement that England's bishops should
acknowledge the king as overlord of their
(immense) secular holdings. By marrying his

daughter to Geoffrey of Anjou, he laid the basis
for a much enlarged kingdom. Henry died in
France of a fever, apparently triggered by a surfeit
of lampreys.

Silver penny of Stephen,
minted at Stafford

Royal coat of arms, Stephen

STEPHEN 1135-1154
Authority King of England, Count of Boulogne,
with claims on Normandy (until 1145)
Dynasty House of Blois
Parents Stephen, Count of Blois and Chartres, and
Adela, fifth daughter of William I the Conqueror,
their third son
Born Blois about 1097
Succeeded to throne 22 Dec 1135
Crowned Westminster Abbey 26 Dec 1135
Reigned 18 years, 307 days
Died St Martin's Priory, Dover, Kent 25 Oct 1154
Buried Faversham Abbey, Kent
Married Matilda of Boulogne (c1103-1152) daughter
of Count Eustace II of Boulogne, 1125
Children Five, notably eldest son Eustace, Count
of Boulogne (c1126-53)

Key facts Stephen usurped the throne and plunged England into prolonged civil war, the Anarchy.

As Henry's I's favourite nephew, Stephen received extensive lands in England and France. He was sworn to accept Henry's daughter Matilda as Henry's successor, but when Henry died Stephen landed in England and claimed the throne. He won backing from nobles rejecting rule by a woman, especially one married to an Angevin (a member of the House of Anjou). But Stephen lacked political judgement and made enemies. Matilda's illegitimate half brother the 1st Earl of Gloucester rebelled, and civil war started in 1139 when Matilda invaded. In April 1141 hostile troops seized Stephen at the Battle of Lincoln but in November exchanged him for Gloucester who had been imprisoned by Stephen's supporters. Stephen then regained much lost power and in 1148 Matilda left England. Stephen named Eustace as his successor, but Matilda's son Henry of Anjou invaded in 1153 and Eustace died. Stephen reluctantly declared Henry his heir.

Good-natured and militarily energetic, Stephen made concessions that failed to win total support. He had to employ lawless and unpopular Flemish mercenaries. He died of a heart attack.

MATILDA 1141
Nicknames Empress Maud
Authority Queen of England (briefly and uncrowned)
Dynasty House of Anjou

Matilda presents a charter

Parents Henry I and Matilda of Scotland, their only daughter
Born London, Feb 1102
Succeeded to throne Apr 1141
Reigned Seven months
Died near Rouen 10 Sept 1167
Buried Fontevrault Abbey, Maine, France
Married (1) Holy Roman Emperor Henry V (1081-1125) 1114 and (2) Geoffrey IV the Handsome, 9th Count of Anjou (1113-1151) 2 June 1129
Children Three sons (by 2), notably Henry II

Key facts Matilda fought Stephen in a long and destructive civil war for the crown of England.

Henry I's heir and the widow of Emperor Henry V, the Empress Matilda married Geoffrey of Anjou as part of Henry I's plan to add to his Norman holdings in France. Matilda invaded England and fought (1139-48) to wrest rule from her usurping cousin Stephen. She won much of the west, and after Stephen's capture in April 1141 a clerical council proclaimed Matilda 'Lady of the English'. She entered London but made cash demands that provoked Londoners to expel her before a coronation. On Stephen's release, she suffered defeats (fled from Oxford Castle Dec 1142), and eventually left England for Normandy, now controlled by her husband. The cause of Matilda's death is obscure.

Although Matilda failed to secure the English throne she laid a basis for successful claims by descendants of her husband Geoffrey of Anjou. Geoffrey's nickname Plantagenet became an unofficial alternative name for the Angevins, England's longest reigning dynasty, established by Matilda's son Henry II. Taken from the Latin *planta genista* ('broom plant'), Plantagenet may refer to a sprig of broom that Geoffrey wore in his hat.

The House of Anjou (Plantagenet) 1154-1485

The Angevin dynasty began with Henry II: son of Geoffrey IV the Handsome, 9th Count of Anjou (in NW France) and Matilda, daughter of England's Henry I. Since the 1400s this dynasty has also borne the name Plantagenet from a supposed nickname of Geoffrey. With Richard II's deposition (1399) the dynasty split into the houses of Lancaster (reigned 1399-1461 and 1470-1) and York (1461-70 and 1471-85). Angevin kings once ruled much of France, but eventually lost all their French possessions, except Calais, in the Hundred Years' War (1337-1453). Family rivalry then sparked off the disastrous Wars of the Roses (1455-85). Angevin rule ended with Richard III's death in battle.

HENRY II 1154-1189
Nicknames Curtmantel (wore a short cloak), Fitz-Empress (son of Empress Matilda)
Authority King of England, overlord of Wales, Scotland, eastern Ireland, and western France.
Dynasty House of Anjou or Plantagenet
Parents Count Geoffrey V of Anjou and Matilda, daughter of Henry I of England, their eldest son
Born Le Mans, Maine 5 Mar 1133
Succeeded to throne 25 Oct 1154
Crowned Westminster Abbey 19 Dec 1154

THE HOUSE OF ANJOU (PLANTAGENET) PART I 1154-1327 (continued next page)

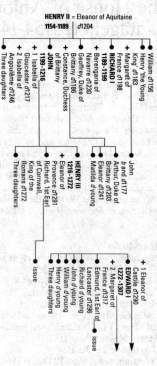

HENRY II = Eleanor of Aquitaine
1154-1189   *d*1204

- William *d*1156
- Henry 'the Young King' *d*1183
- + Margaret of France *d*1198
- **RICHARD I**
  1189-1199
  + Berengaria of Navarre *d*1230
- Geoffrey, Duke of Brittany *d*1186
  + Constance, Duchess of Brittany
- **JOHN**
  1199-1216
  + 1 Isabella of Gloucester *d*1217
  + 2 Isabella of Angoulême *d*1246
  - Three daughters
- John *b* and *d*1177
- Arthur, Duke of Brittany *d*1203
- Eleanor *d*1241
- Matilda *d* young

- **HENRY III**
  1216-1272
  + Eleanor of Provence *d*1291
- Richard, 1st Earl of Cornwall, King of the Romans *d*1272
  - Three daughters
  - issue

- **EDWARD I**
  1272-1307
  + 1 Eleanor of Castile *d*1290
  + 2 Margaret of France *d*1317
  - Edmund, 1st Earl of Lancaster *d*1296
  - Richard *d* young
  - John *d* young
  - William *d* young
  - Henry *d* young
  - Three daughters
  - issue

THE HOUSE OF ANJOU (PLANTAGENET) PART I 1154-1327 (continued)

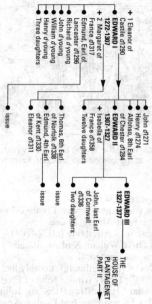

John d1271
Henry d1274
Alfonso, 8th Earl
of Chester d1284

+ 1 Eleanor of
Castile d1290
EDWARD I
1272-1307

+ 2 Margaret of
France d1311
Edmund, Earl of
Lancaster d1296
Richard d'young
John d'young
Henry d'young
William d'young
Three daughters

+ Isabella of
France d1358
EDWARD II
1307-1327
Twelve daughters

Thomas, 6th Earl
of Norfolk d1338
Edmund, 4th Earl
of Kent d1330
Eleanor d1311

EDWARD III
1327-1377
John, last Earl
of Cornwall
d1336
Two daughters

THE
HOUSE OF
PLANTAGENET
PART II

issue

issue

issue

Coronation of Henry the Young King 1170 whom Henry II then serves at the coronation banquet, French MS 1230-60

Reigned 34 years, 254 days
Died Chinon Castle, near Tours, France 6 July 1189
Buried Fontevrault Abbey, Maine
Married Eleanor of Aquitaine (c1122-1204), daughter of Duke William X of Aquitaine 18 May 1152 at Bordeaux Cathedral
Children Eleven (3 illegitimate), notably five sons: William (1153-6); Henry (titular King of England 1170-83); Richard I; Geoffrey (1158-86); John
Key facts This French-born first English Angevin or Plantagenet king proved an outstanding medieval monarch who strengthened royal administration and ruled from Scotland to the Pyrenees.

Henry II debates with
Archbishop Becket, from Peter
of Longtoft's 14th century
Chronicle of England

Royal coat of arms, Henry II to
Edward II

Able, energetic, intelligent, and ruthless, he worked to curb nobles' powers (over 70 castles demolished or confiscated)and the authority of the Church. He reformed English law and built a royal bureaucracy. By war and diplomacy he mastered more of Europe than any other English monarch. Henry inherited England, Anjou (1151), Maine, Normandy (1149) and Touraine; acquired Aquitaine, Gascony, Poitou, and Brittany by dynastic marriages; and, partly by war, laid claim to Ireland, Scotland, and Wales. He spent only 14 years in England.

Henry's law reforms introduced circuit courts and trial by jury, and established Anglo-Saxon common law as the law of England. However his conflict with the bishops led four knights to murder Henry's old friend and ex-chancellor Thomas à Becket, Archbishop of Canterbury (1170), and Henry's divide-and-rule policy led to frequent and ultimately successful revolts by his sons Richard and John. Henry died in France of a fever, a beaten monarch.

RICHARD I 1189-1199
Nicknames Coeur de Lion (Lionheart)
Authority King of England and ruler of western France
Dynasty House of Anjou or Plantagenet
Parents Henry II and Eleanor of Aquitaine, their third son
Born Beaumont Palace, Oxford 8 Sept 1157
Succeeded to throne 6 July 1189

Crowned Westminster Abbey 3 Sept 1189
Reigned 9 years, 274 days
Died Châlus, Limousin 6 Apr 1199
Buried Fontevrault Abbey (heart in Rouen);
reburied Westminster Abbey
Married Berengaria of Navarre (died after 1230),
daughter of King Sancho VI of Navarre, 12 May
1191 at Chapel of St George, Limassol, Cyprus
Children An acknowledged illegitimate son

Richard I is arrested in Austria despite his disguise as
a woodsman 20 Dec 1192, from *Chronicle of Petrus de
Eboli*

Key facts Richard I was an Angevin warrior king
who spent only six months of his reign in England.

Twice rebelling as Duke of Aquitaine against his
father in France (1173-4 and 1188-9), he eventually
sided with King Philip II of France for a war in
which Henry died. With other Christian leaders, in
1189 Richard launched the Third Crusade against
Muslim rule in the Holy Land. He conquered
Cyprus (1191), retook Acre and Jaffa, failed to
retake Jerusalem from Saladin, yet secured
Christian access to the holy places.

Richard antagonized fellow crusaders, and
Leopold V, Duke of Austria, seized him in Vienna
on his way home. Richard spent 17 months
imprisoned in castles controlled by the Emperor
Henry VI. An unlikely legend describes him being
found when his favourite minstrel Blondel sang
below a castle wall. Ransomed for three times his
annual income in 1194, Richard briefly visited
England, which he left in the Archbishop of
Canterbury's capable hands. He spent his last five
years fighting Philip II in France, and died of a
shoulder wound while besieging a castle.

Richard I was brave, cruel, and generous, and
inspired loyalty. He was a superb military leader
and a fine troubadour-style lyric poet, but his wars
drained England of money and weakened the
crown. He may have been bisexual.

JOHN 1199-1216

Nicknames Lackland (Sans Terre), Sword of Lath ('Softsword')

Authority King of England with claims to rule Ireland (Lord from 1185), Scotland, Wales, and western France.

Dynasty House of Anjou or Plantagenet

Parents Henry II and Eleanor of Aquitaine, their youngest son

Born Beaumont Palace, Oxford 24 Dec 1167

Succeeded to throne 6 Apr 1199

Crowned Westminster Abbey 27 May 1199

Reigned 17 years, 195 days

Preamble to Magna Carta with John's royal titles and episcopal/baronial witnesses 15 June 1215

Died Newark Castle, Nottinghamshire 18 Oct 1216
Buried Worcester Cathdral
Married (1) Isabella of Gloucester (died 1217) 29
Aug 1189 at Marlborough, Wiltshire and (2)
Isabella of Angoulême (died 1246), daughter of
Count Audemar of Angoulême, 26 August 1200 at
Angoulême
Children Five by (2), notably Henry III, Richard
(1209-72), Isabella (1210-38), and Eleanor (1215-
75), and five illegitimate
Key facts Henry II's youngest son, John was a
skilled politician and forceful administrator, but
one of England's most unpopular monarchs due to
his cruelty and deceit.

While Richard I was imprisoned abroad, in 1193
John vainly bid to usurp the throne. He was
banished, but soon reconciled and made his
brother's heir. On Richard's death John became
king and imprisoned his young nephew Arthur of
Brittany, a better claimant who soon died in gaol.
Wars with Philip II of France (1202-4 and 1213-14)
cost John north-west France, above all his Duchy
of Normandy (except the Channel Islands). John's
refusal to accept Stephen Langton, Pope Innocent
III's nominee, as Archbishop of Canterbury led the
Pope to close England's churches and
excommunicate John (1208-9), forcing him to give
way.

John asserted his power in Ireland, Scotland,
and Wales, but costly wars and cavalier treatment
of his barons provoked civil war. In 1215 John
reluctantly accepted the Magna Carta (Great

Charter), outlining royal powers and the rights of barons and freemen. He died of dysentery fighting a renewed civil war.

Henry III carries the Holy Blood to Westminster, 1247 (drawing by his chronicler Matthew Paris c1200-59)

HENRY III 1216-1272
Authority King of England with claims on Ireland, Scotland, Wales, and south-west France (Duke of Aquitaine)
Dynasty House of Anjou or Plantagenet
Parents King John and Isabella of Angoulême, their eldest son
Born Winchester, Hampshire 1 Oct 1207
Succeeded to throne 18 Oct 1216
Crowned Gloucester Cathedral 28 Oct 1216 and at Westminster Abbey 17 May 1220
Reigned 56 years, 29 days

Henry III sails home from Gascony 1243 (drawing by his chronicler Matthew Paris c1200-59)

Died Westminster Palace, London 16 Nov 1272
Buried Westminster Abbey
Married Eleanor of Provence (died 1291), daughter of Count Raymond Berengar IV of Provence, 20 Jan 1236 at Canterbury
Children At least nine, notably Edward I, Margaret (1240-75) and Edmund Crouchback (1245-96)
Key facts Henry's incompetence at ruling indirectly helped create an English Parliament.

Inheriting the throne aged only nine, Henry ruled ineffectually and extravagantly from 1227 through friends and relatives. Wales got out of hand and Henry failed to retake Poitou and Anjou, becoming the only English king to be defeated in battle by a French one. Such costly ventures drove Henry to appeal for cash to his barons, who forced him to accept far-reaching reforms in the Provisions of Oxford (1258). These established a baronially- dominated privy council to oversee administration.

Henry renounced the provisions in 1264, provoking the Barons' War led by his brother-in-law Simon de Montfort who captured Henry at the Battle of Lewes and formed the first parliament with representatives from towns. Henry's son Edward defeated and killed de Montfort at the Battle of Evesham (1265) and became effective ruler. Henry lived another seven years, to complete Westminster Abbey's rebuilding, but he was now weak and senile.

Henry III had proved ambitious and cultured, but arrogant, impractical, and cowardly. His weakness had helped strengthen demands for an established legal system and regularized political dealings between monarch and nobles. As early as 1240 the King's Great Council became known as Parliament.

EDWARD I 1272-1307
Nicknames Longshanks (long legs), Hammer of the Scots (16th century inscription on his tomb), the Lawgiver, the English Justinian
Authority King of England, Wales, Scotland, and Ireland, the Isle of Man (from 1290) and ruler in south-west France (Duke of Aquitaine)
Dynasty House of Plantagenet
Parents Henry III and Eleanor of Provence, their eldest surviving son

Born Westminster Palace 17 June 1239
Succeeded to the throne 20 Nov 1272
Crowned Westminster Abbey 18 August 1274
Reigned 34 years, 224 days
Died Burgh-by-Sands, near Carlisle 7 July 1307
Buried Westminster Abbey
Married (1) Eleanor of Castile (c1244-90), daughter
of King Ferdinand III of Castile, Oct 1254 at Las
Huelgas monastery, Spain and (2) Margaret of
France (1282-1317), daughter of King Philip III of
France, at Canterbury 10 Sept 1299
Children Sixteen by Eleanor, notably Joan (1272-
1307), Margaret (1275-1318), Elizabeth, and
Edward II; and three by Margaret, notably
Thomas of Brotherton (1300-38) and Edmund of
Woodstock (died 1330)
Key facts The first truly English king, Edward
proved a masterful ruler, military genius and great
legislator, taking advice from able lawyers and
ministers.

To raise cash for government and the army in
1295, Edward called the Model Parliament.
Representing nobles, Church, and commoners, this
foreshadowed representative government and
decreed that the King needed Parliament's
approval to make laws or raise non-feudal taxes.
Edward backed laws curbing Church power and
curtailing feudal rights. Under Edward, the great
common law courts (King's Bench, Exchequer,
Common Pleas) took shape.

Edward forcefully stamped his authority on
Wales and Scotland. He invaded Wales, killing

Edward I from his Memorandum Roll 1297/8

Hardingstone Eleanor Cross (Northants), one of 12 erected in 1291-4 by Edward to his beloved first wife

Welsh princes, establishing English control (1277-83) with the aid of nine new castles. On 7 February 1301 he created the title Prince of Wales for his fourth son, born at Caernarvon Castle. From 1296 to his death, Edward fought wars to conquer Scotland. He defeated John de Balliol (1296) and William Wallace (1298) but died on his way to subdue Robert the Bruce.

Edward II surrenders his crown to his son Edward III 1327, from Peter Langtoft's contemporary *Chronicle*

EDWARD II 1307–1327
Nickname Edward of Caernarvon
Authority King of England and Wales, with claims on Ireland, Scotland, the Isle of Man (until 1313) and south-west France (Duke of Aquitaine)
Dynasty House of Plantagenet

Parents Edward I and Eleanor of Castile, their fourth son
Born Caernarvon Castle, North Wales 25 Apr 1284
Succeeded to throne 7 July 1307
Crowned Westminster Abbey 25 Feb 1308
Reigned 19 years, 197 days
Abdicated 20 Jan 1327 at Kenilworth, Warwickshire
Died Berkeley Castle, Gloucestershire 21 Sept 1327
Buried Gloucester Cathedral
Married Isabella (1292-1358), daughter of King Philip III of France, 25 January 1308 at Boulogne
Children Four, notably Edward III
Key facts Edward II was an effete and incompetent ruler who intermittently and unsuccessfully fought to subdue dissident barons and Scottish nationalists.

Edward became the first English Prince of Wales in 1301. As king, he antagonized powerful nobles by granting favours to personal favourites Piers Gaveston and, later, Hugh le Despenser father and son. By the Ordinances of 1311, barons forced Edward to banish Gaveston and executed him (1312) when Edward let him return. Later, Edward's cousin the powerful Thomas of Lancaster banished the Despensers but was captured and killed by Edward (1322).

Meanwhile, international problems arose. In 1314 Robert the Bruce's Scottish army crushed Edward's troops at Bannockburn, winning independence for Scotland. In 1324-5 French troops for a while overran Edward's Duchy of

Edward II and Queen Isabella, from Walter de Millimete's 1326 treatise *On the Duties of Kings* presented to Prince Edward (III)

Aquitaine in south-west France. Last, in 1326 Edward's exiled baronial opponent Roger Mortimer invaded England from France with his mistress, Edward's disaffected 'She-Wolf' wife Isabella. The invaders hanged the Despensers, deposed Edward, and crowned his son king. Edward soon died in prison, reputedly disembowelled by a red-hot iron.

EDWARD III 1327-1377
Nicknames Edward of Windsor, 'King of the Sea'
Authority King of England and Wales, with claims over Ireland, Scotland and Isle of Man (from 1333), and France (from 1340)
Dynasty House of Plantagenet
Parents Edward II and Isabella of France, their elder son

Edward III's French lands 1360-9

Born Windsor Castle, Berks 13 Nov 1312
Succeeded to throne 25 Jan 1327
Crowned Westminster Abbey 29 Jan 1327
Reigned 50 years, 147 days
Died Sheen Palace, Surrey 21 June 1377
Buried Westminster Abbey
Married Philippa of Hainault (c1314-69), daughter of Count William I of Hainault and Holland, 24 Jan 1328 at York
Children Twelve, notably Edward the Black Prince (1330-76), Lionel of Antwerp (1338-68), John of Gaunt (1340-99), Thomas of Woodstock (1355-97) and Edmund of Langley (1341-1402)
Key facts Edward III was an affable, majestic king

Royal coat of arms
of Edward III 1337

Tomb effigy of Edward III

and superb military commander, leading Europe's
finest army and fleet in prolonged wars against
France and Scotland.

Aged only 14 at accession, he began his active
rule in 1330 after killing Roger Mortimer who had
ruled in his name. Edward determined to rebuild
England's international power. He failed to secure
Scotland but launched the Hundred Years' War
(1337-1453). In 1338 he ravaged northern and
eastern France and proclaimed himself King of
France (1340), a title boasted by all English
monarchs until 1801. However, victories at Sluys
(1340), Crécy (1346), Calais (1347), Winchelsea
(1350) and, his son's at Poitiers (1356), ultimately
added only Calais as a long-lasting English
possession.

THE HOUSE OF ANJOU
(PLANTAGENET) PART II 1327-1399

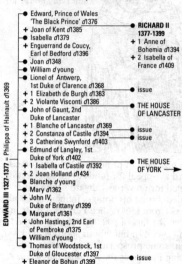

EDWARD III 1327-1377 = Philippa of Hainault d1369

- Edward, Prince of Wales 'The Black Prince' d1376
- + Joan of Kent d1385 → **RICHARD II 1377-1399**
  - + 1 Anne of Bohemia d1394
  - + 2 Isabella of France d1409
- Isabella d1379
- + Enguerrand de Coucy, Earl of Bedford d1396
- Joan d1348
- William d young
- Lionel of Antwerp, 1st Duke of Clarence d1368
- + 1 Elizabeth de Burgh d1363 → issue
- + 2 Violante Visconti d1386
- John of Gaunt, 2nd Duke of Lancaster → **THE HOUSE OF LANCASTER**
- + 1 Blanche of Lancaster d1369 → issue
- + 2 Constanza of Castile d1394 → issue
- + 3 Catherine Swynford d1403
- Edmund of Langley, 1st Duke of York d1402
- + 1 Isabella of Castile d1392 → **THE HOUSE OF YORK →**
- + 2 Joan Holland d1434
- Blanche d young
- Mary d1362
- + John IV, Duke of Brittany d1399
- Margaret d1361
- + John Hastings, 2nd Earl of Pembroke d1375
- William d young
- Thomas of Woodstock, 1st Duke of Gloucester d1397 → issue
- + Eleanor de Bohun d1399

Edward III and
Philip VI of France
meet 1331, French
late 14th century MS

The high cost of prolonged fighting forced
Edward to appeal for funds to his nobles, who
struggled for power as Edward's authority
dwindled during his dotage, influenced by his
mistress (from 1364) Alice Perrers. Other problems
included the loss of 800,000 subjects to the Black
Death (1348-49), but labour shortage and war
brought some prosperity. English was now
replacing French as the national language. Among
institutions, justices of the peace were so titled in
1360, Edward founded the Order of the Garter
(1348) and his parliaments, first divided into Lords
and Commons (1332), became fixed at
Westminster, using English from 1362.

RICHARD II 1377-1399
Nicknames Richard of Bordeaux
Authority King of England and Wales, with claims over Ireland and France
Dynasty House of Plantagenet
Parents Edward the Black Prince and Joan of Kent, their second, only surviving son
Born Bordeaux 6 Jan 1367
Succeeded to throne 22 June 1367
Crowned Westminster Abbey 16 July 1377
Reigned 22 years, 99 days
Abdicated 29 Sept 1399 at Tower of London
Died Pontefract Castle, Yorks 14 Feb 1400
Buried Kings Langley, Herts, reburied Westminster Abbey 1413
Married (1) Anne of Bohemia (1366-94), daughter of Emperor Charles IV, 20 Jan 1382 at St Stephen's Chapel, Westminster and (2) Isabella (1389-1409), daughter of King Charles VI of France, 4 Nov 1396 at St Nicholas' Chapel, Westminster
Children None

Royal coat of arms, Richard II incorporating Edward the Confessor's supposed arms (left side)

Key facts Richard proved tyrannical but ineffectual in his struggle to assert royal authority.

A grandson of Edward III, and nephew of John of Gaunt, 2nd Duke of Lancaster, Richard came to the throne aged only 10. John of Gaunt wielded the real power. Gaunt's misrule, the costly Hundred Years' War with France (1337-1453), the aftermath of the Black Death and a poll tax all contributed to spark off the Peasants' Revolt (1381) put down by Richard with spirit and guile. Powerful enemies among the nobility curbed Richard's powers while Gaunt was abroad, but Richard later won royalist backers and killed or banished leading opponents (1397-8). However, while he visited Ireland the now dead John of Gaunt's exiled son Henry of Bolingbroke landed in England (July 1399) and rallied nobles angered by Richard's ruthless taxation and efforts to limit their powers. Richard returned, surrendered to Henry, and abdicated in Henry's favour. Richard was imprisoned in Pontefract Castle where he died, murdered or from self-inflicted starvation.

Richard had been a good judge of literature, patronizing the poets Geoffrey Chaucer and John Gower, and the chronicler Jean Froissart. In fashion he is said to have introduced the handkerchief.

HENRY IV 1399-1413
Nickname Henry of Bolingbroke
Authority King of England and Wales, with claims over France and Ireland,

Royal coat of arms, Henry IV to Elizabeth I

Henry IV invests Richard Beauchamp, 13th Earl of Warwick (1382-1439), with the Order of the Garter 1410 (from a silverpoint drawing c1485-90)

THE HOUSE OF LANCASTER 1399-1471

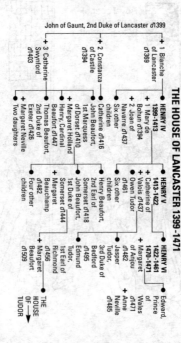

John of Gaunt, 2nd Duke of Lancaster d1399

+ 1 Blanche of Lancaster d1369

+ 2 Constanza of Castile d1394

+ 3 Catherine Swynford d1403

HENRY IV 1399-1413
+ 1 Mary de Bohun d1394
+ 2 Joan of Navarre d1437
• Six other children
• Catherine d1416
• John Beaufort, 1st Marquess of Dorset d1410
• Henry, Cardinal Beaufort d1447
• Thomas Beaufort, Duke of Exeter d1426
+ Margaret Neville

HENRY V 1413-1422
+ Catherine of Valois d1437
+ Owen Tudor
• Six other children
• Henry Beaufort, 2nd Earl of Somerset d1418
• John Beaufort, 1st Duke of Somerset d1444
+ Margaret Beauchamp
• Two daughters
• Four other children

HENRY VI 1422-1461 1470-1471
+ Margaret of Anjou d1482
• Jasper Tudor, 3rd Duke of Bedford d1495
• Edmund Tudor, 1st Earl of Richmond d1456
+ Margaret Beaufort d1509

• Edward, Prince of Wales d1471
+ Anne Neville d1485

THE HOUSE OF TUDOR →

Dynasty House of Lancaster
Parents John of Gaunt and Blanche of Lancaster
(John's cousin), their eldest son
Born Bolingbroke Castle, Lincs April 1366
Succeeded to the throne 30 Sept 1399
Crowned Westminster Abbey 13 Oct 1399
Reigned 13 years, 171 days
Died Jerusalem Chamber, Westminster Palace 20
Mar 1413
Buried Canterbury Cathedral
Married (1) Mary de Bohun (1368/70-94), daughter
of Humphrey X, Earl of Hereford, 1380 or 1381 at
Rochford, Essex and (2) Joan of Navarre (c1370-
1437), daughter of King Charles II of Navarre 7
Feb 1403 at Winchester
Children Seven by (1) notably Henry V
Key facts Eldest surviving son of John of Gaunt,
2nd Duke of Lancaster (1340-99). Henry usurped
the throne and became the first king of the House
of Lancaster.

As Henry of Bolingbroke, in the 1380s he had
joined nobles who curbed Richard II's authority.
Later he joined crusades in Lithuania and Prussia
(1390-2). In 1398 Richard banished Henry and on
John of Gaunt's death seized Lancastrian estates.
To reclaim this inheritance, Henry invaded (1399),
forced Richard's abdication, and (as a descendant
of Henry III) had Parliament recognize himself as
king.

Plots and revolts bedevilled his reign. Henry
crushed a pro-Richard rising (1400); campaigned
(1400-5) in Wales against Owen Glendower;

smashed the rebellious Percies of Northumberland at Shrewsbury (1403); suppressed Archbishop (of York) Scrope's rebellion (1405); and faced incursions by Scots and French. Parliament secured concessions in return for cash grants to pay for these struggles.

Henry encouraged the growth of towns and trade but suppressed Lollard religious dissidents. The King reputedly suffered from epilepsy and supposedly died of leprosy, syphilis, or, more probably a severe form of eczema combined with gout.

HENRY V 1413-1422
Nickname Henry of Monmouth
Authority King of England and Wales, ruling parts of Ireland and France (Regent, 1420), Duke of Normandy (from 1417)
Dynasty House of Lancaster
Parents Henry IV and Mary de Bohun, their second and surviving son
Born Monmouth 9 Aug or 16 Sept 1387
Succeeded to throne 20 Mar 1413
Crowned Westminster Abbey 9 Apr 1413
Reigned 9 years, 164 days
Died Vincennes Castle, near Paris, 31 Aug 1422
Buried Chapel of the Confessor, Westminster Abbey
Married Catherine of Valois (1401-37), youngest daughter of King Charles VI of France 2 June 1420 at St John's Church, Troyes
Children Henry VI

Henry V's
standard

The marriage of Henry V and Catherine of Valois, 1420
(from a silverpoint drawing c1485-90)

Key facts An able, popular leader, Henry
transformed England briefly into the strongest
nation in Europe.

As Prince of Wales he had fought against Welsh
rebels (1403-8). When he became king, youthful
high spirits gave way to ardent ambition. Henry
swiftly crushed domestic plots, then reasserted the
English monarchy's claim to rule France. Henry
revived the Hundred Years' War, winning the
Battle of Agincourt (1415), reconquering
Normandy (1417-19), reaching Paris (1419), and
securing the Treaty of Troyes (1420) which
recognized Henry as heir to the French throne and

Henry V at the Siege of Rouen 1418-19 (from a
silverpoint drawing c1485-90)

Regent of France. Henry died of dysentery in France while defending these claims.

Skilled planning and able lieutenants had underpinned Henry's military triumphs. Personal popularity helped him raise cash at home to pay for the war. Henry's diplomacy deprived France of powerful allies, Henry's ships dominated the English Channel, and his English garrisons made northern French towns strongholds controlling the countryside.

Henry was brave and loyal, with a commanding presence, but harsh and ruthless in achieving his goals. At home these included burning religious dissidents, but there was little time for constructive domestic reforms.

HENRY VI 1422-1461, 1470-1471

Authority King of England and Wales, with control of parts of France (till 1453) and Ireland
Dynasty House of Lancaster
Parents Henry V and Catherine of Valois, their only child
Born Windsor Castle 6 Dec 1421
Succeeded to throne 1 Sept 1422
Crowned Westminster Abbey 6 Nov 1429, St Denis, Paris 16 Dec 1431; St Paul's Cathedral 13 Oct 1470
Reigned 38 years, 184 days; 187 days (1470-1)
Deposed 4 Mar 1461 (Restored 3 Oct 1470) and 11 Apr 1471
Died Tower of London 21 May 1471
Buried Chertsey Abbey, reburied St George's

Chapel, Windsor Castle (1484)
Married Margaret of Anjou (1430-82), daughter of
Duke René of Anjou, 23 Apr 1445 at Tichfield
Abbey, New Forest near Southampton
Children Edward, Prince of Wales (1453-71)
Key facts Henry VI was a scholarly, pious king,
who became a pawn in the Wars of the Roses
(1455-85).

Henry was only nine months old when he
became King of England, and a month later was
acclaimed King of France. His minority ended in
1437 and he was soon founding famous educational
establishments such as King's College, Cambridge
(1441). True power, though, lay with rival ministers
of the Houses of York and Lancaster, notably
Richard, 3rd Duke of York, and Edmund
Beaufort, 2nd Duke of Somerset, descendants of
Edward III.

After Henry suffered a phase of insanity
(1453-4), fighting broke out between both factions,
later symbolized by badges depicting the white rose
of York and the red rose of Lancaster. The pacifist
Henry was seized by Yorkists (1460) and forced to
acknowledge York as his heir. Lancastrians
recaptured Henry (1461) but Yorkists declared him
deposed. Henry again fell into Yorkist hands
(1465), but was briefly (1470-1) restored to the
throne by former Yorkist supporter Richard
Neville, 15th Earl of Warwick, who governed in
Henry's name. In May 1471 Richard of York's son
Edward IV defeated and killed Warwick and
Henry's son, and had Henry murdered.

The infant Henry VI held in Parliament by his guardian,
Richard Beauchamp, 13th Earl of Warwick, 1428
(from a silverpoint drawing c1485-90)

THE HOUSE OF YORK 1461-1485 (continued next page)

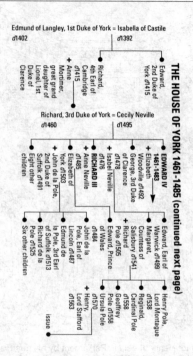

Edmund of Langley, 1st Duke of York = Isabella of Castile
*d*1402   *d*1392

- Edward, 2nd Duke of York *d*1415
- Richard, 4th Earl of Cambridge *d*1415
  + Anne Mortimer, great grand daughter of Lionel, 1st Duke of Clarence

Richard, 3rd Duke of York = Cecily Neville
*d*1460   *d*1495

- **EDWARD IV 1461-1483**
  + Elizabeth Woodville *d*1492
  - Edward, Prince of Wales *d*1484
  - Elizabeth of York *d*1503
    + Henry, Lord Stafford *d*1563
  - issue
- George, 3rd Duke of Clarence *d*1478
  + Isabel Neville *d*1476
  - Edward, Earl of Warwick *d*1499
  - Margaret, Countess of Salisbury *d*1541
    + Richard Pole *d*1505
    - Henry, Lord Montague *d*1538
    - Reginald, Cardinal Pole *d*1558
    - Geoffrey Pole *d*1558
    - Ursula Pole *d*1570
- **RICHARD III**
  + Anne Neville *d*1485
- John de la Pole, 2nd Duke of Suffolk *d*1491
  - John de la Pole, Earl of Lincoln *d*1487
  - Edmund de la Pole, 3rd Earl of Suffolk *d*1513
  - Richard de la Pole *d*1525
  - Six other children
- Eight other children

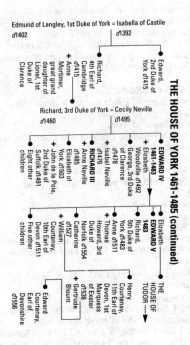

THE HOUSE OF YORK 1461-1485 (continued)

Edmund of Langley, 1st Duke of York *d*1402 = Isabella of Castile *d*1392

+ Richard, 4th Earl of Cambridge *d*1415
+ Anne Mortimer, great grand daughter of Lionel, 1st Duke of Clarence

Edward, 2nd Duke of York *d*1415

Richard, 3rd Duke of York *d*1460 = Cecily Neville *d*1495

EDWARD IV 1461-1483
+ Elizabeth Woodville *d*1492

George, 3rd Duke of Clarence *d*1478
+ Isabel Neville *d*1476

RICHARD III *d*1485
+ Anne Neville *d*1485

Elizabeth of York *d*1503
+ John de la Pole, 2nd Duke of Suffolk *d*1491

Eight other children

EDWARD V 1483

Richard, 5th Duke of York *d*1483

Anne *d*1511
+ Thomas Howard, 3rd Duke of Norfolk *d*1554

Catherine *d*1527
+ William Courtenay, 10th Earl of Devon *d*1511

Five other children

Henry Courtenay, 11th Earl of Devon, 1st Marquess of Exeter *d*1538
+ Gertrude Blount

Edward Courtenay, Earl of Devonshire *d*1556

Elizabeth = THE HOUSE OF TUDOR →

His reign had earlier survived Jack Cade's Kentish Rebellion (1450), but had seen the loss of all France except Calais to the French resurgence, begun by Joan of Arc. This culminated in the conquests of Normandy and Gascony that ended the Hundred Years' War.

EDWARD IV 1461-1483
Authority King of England and Wales, ruling Calais and part of Ireland
Dynasty House of York
Parents Richard, 3rd Duke of York and Cicely, daughter of Ralph Neville, 1st Earl of Westmoreland, their eldest son
Born Rouen, France 28 Apr 1442
Succeeded to the throne (1) 4 Mar 1461 and (2) 11 Apr 1471
Crowned Westminster Abbey 28 June 1461
Reigned 22 years, 36 days
Died Westminster Palace 9 Apr 1483
Married Elizabeth Woodville (c1437-92), daughter of Sir Richard Neville, 1 May 1464 at Grafton, Northants
Children Ten, notably Elizabeth, Edward V, Richard
Key facts Edward was the first Yorkist king, ousting Lancastrian Henry VI in the dynastic civil wars later called the Wars of the Roses.

On 2 Feb 1461 the 18-year-old Edward led an army that crushed the Lancastrians at Mortimer's Cross avenging the recent death of his father 'the Protector' Richard, Duke of York, a claimant to

Edward IV drawn on the King's Bench Plea Roll, Hilary Term 1466

the throne. Edward had himself crowned, and drove the deposed Henry north into Scotland. Friction later arose between Edward and his cousin Richard Neville, 15th Earl of Warwick, called the Kingmaker (1428-71) for his powerful role in supporting the Yorkist bid for the throne. Warwick rebelled (1469), and allying with Henry VI's influential wife Queen Margaret forced Edward to flee the realm. They deposed Edward (3 Oct 1470) but with 1200 mercenaries the King returned from Holland to crush Warwick at Barnet (14 Apr 1471) and Margaret at Tewkesbury (4 May 1471), killing her son, then murdering Henry VI.

His throne now secure from Lancastrian attack, Edward invaded France (1475), but was paid off and withdrew. Financially skilled, he encouraged trade, especially in wool, and was the first solvent monarch at his death since 1189. In his 'second' reign law enforcement also improved, and England enjoyed increased prosperity.

EDWARD V 1483
Authority as Edward IV
Dynasty House of York
Parents Edward IV and Elizabeth (Woodville)
Born Abbot's house, Westminster 2 Nov 1470
Succeeded to throne 9 Apr 1483 (not crowned)
Reigned 77 days
Deposed 25 June 1483
Died Tower of London ?Sept 1483
Key facts Within weeks of becoming king, Edward fell victim to an uncle's ambition for power.

Made Prince of Wales during infancy (1471), Edward lived in Ludlow near the Welsh border until he became king, under the power of his mother's family, the Woodvilles. Edward's officially appointed guardian was his uncle Richard, Duke of Gloucester. Fearing the Woodvilles' power, Richard arrested their leaders, killing Edward's grandfather Earl Rivers and an uncle, and forcing Edward's mother, Queen Elizabeth, to seek safety in Westminster Abbey.

Gloucester placed Edward and Edward's nine-year-old younger brother Richard, Duke of York, (born 17 Aug 1473 at Shrewsbury) in the Tower of London, which was then both a royal residence and a prison. Gloucester declared both boys illegitimate (c10 June)on the pretext that Edward IV's (secret) marriage had been invalid. Parliament agreed, and, a day after Edward V should have been crowned, proclaimed Gloucester king, as Richard III.

Princes Edward and Richard vanished, undoubtedly murdered. Their probable remains were found in the Tower of London nearly two centuries later (1674). Both the Little Princes were probably killed by agents of Richard III, or just conceivably by Richard's associate Henry Stafford, 2nd Duke of Buckingham, or by Richard's eventual successor, Henry Tudor, 2nd Earl of Richmond.

RICHARD III 1483-1485

Nicknames Richard Crookback, 'Old Dick'
Authority King of England and Wales, ruling
Calais and part of Ireland
Dynasty House of York
Parents Richard, 3rd Duke of York and Lady
Cecily Neville, their fourth surviving son
Born Fotheringhay Castle, Northants 2 Oct 1452
Succeeded to the throne 26 June 1483
Crowned Westminster Abbey 6 July 1483
Reigned Two years, 57 days
Died Bosworth Field, Leics 22 Aug 1485
Buried Abbey of the Grey Friars, Leicester
Married Anne Neville (1456-85), daughter of
Warwick the Kingmaker, 12 July 1472 at
Westminster Abbey
Children Edward, Prince of Wales (1473-84)
Key facts Richard was the last Yorkist monarch,
who usurped the throne from his nephew and died
in the battle that ended the Wars of the Roses.

Richard ably supported his brother Edward IV
in the 1471 victories over Lancastrian backers of
Edward's rival Henry VI. Edward had already
made Richard the third royal Duke of Gloucester
(1461), and marriage brought him half the immense
Neville estates. In 1480-2, as Lieutenant General in
the North, Richard defended the West Marches,
occupied Edinburgh and retook Berwick from the
Scots.

Edward's death in 1483 left Richard Protector of
the realm, ruling for Edward's young son Edward
V. Richard quickly crushed Edward's mother's

Richard III, stained glass window in Church of St Andrew, Penrith, Cumberland, one of his northern estates

Richard III and Queen Anne, contemporary from Writhe's Garter Book

powerful Woodville relatives, imprisoned Edward, and had himself proclaimed king by Parliament (*see* Edward V). Richard then probably had Edward murdered. Still in 1483, he smashed a revolt by his disaffected associate Henry Stafford, 2nd Duke of Buckingham, and had him beheaded.

Richard then launched financial reforms and boosted trade, but faced growing opposition from nobles resenting his spurious claims to the crown. At the disastrous Battle of Bosworth , Richard died fighting a rival claimant, the Lancastrian Henry Tudor, 2nd Earl of Richmond.

Later Tudor publicity depicted Richard as a deformed villain. Although cruel and cynical, he had proved an able administrator adept at winning popular support, particularly in the North.

The House of Tudor
1485-1603

This dynasty came to power when Henry VII killed Richard III. The name Tudor stemmed from Henry's father Edmund Tudor, 1st Earl of Richmond, the son of Sir Owen Tudor and Henry V's widow Catherine. The Tudors restored order after civil war, formalized Protestantism, and presided over increased trade, exploration, and naval strength that set England on the path to

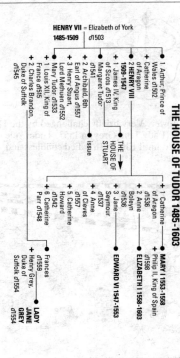

THE HOUSE OF TUDOR 1485-1603

HENRY VII = Elizabeth of York
1485-1509 *d*1503

- 1 Arthur, Prince of Wales *d*1502
- + 2 Catherine of Aragon
- 2 **HENRY VIII** **1509-1547**
- + 1 James IV, King of Scots *d*1513 — Margaret Tudor *d*1541
  - + 2 Archibald, 6th Earl of Angus *d*1557 — THE HOUSE OF STUART
  - + 3 Henry Stuart, Lord Methuen *d*1552
  - issue
- 1 Louis XII, King of France *d*1515 — Mary Tudor *d*1533
  - + 2 Charles Brandon, Duke of Suffolk *d*1545

HENRY VIII married:
- + 1 Catherine of Aragon *d*1536 — **MARY I 1553-1558** + Philip II, King of Spain *d*1598
- + 2 Anne Boleyn *d*1536 — **ELIZABETH I 1558-1603**
- + 3 Jane Seymour *d*1537 — **EDWARD VI 1547-1553**
- + 4 Anne of Cleves *d*1557
- + 5 Catherine Howard *d*1542
- + 6 Catherine Parr *d*1548

Frances *d*1559 + Henry Grey, Duke of Suffolk *d*1554 — **LADY JANE GREY** *d*1554

The Tudor Rose

world power. Very briefly challenged by the House of Grey (Lady Jane Grey)in 1553, Tudor rule continued until Elizabeth I died childless and unmarried.

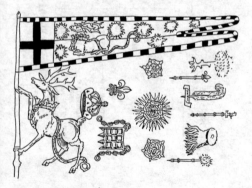

Henry VII's standard with other Tudor emblems and regalia

HENRY VII 1485-1509
Authority King of England and Wales, ruling
Calais and part of Ireland
Dynasty House of Tudor
Parents Edmund Tudor, 1st Earl of Richmond and
Margaret Beaufort, great-great granddaughter of
Edward III, their only child
Born Pembroke Castle, Wales 28 Jan 1457
Succeeded to the throne 22 Aug 1485
Crowned Westminster Abbey 30 Oct 1485
Reigned 23 years, 242 days
Died Richmond Palace, Surrey 21 Apr 1509
Buried Henry VII's Chapel, Westminster Abbey
Married Elizabeth of York (1466-1503), eldest
daughter of Edward IV, 18 Jan 1486 at
Westminster Abbey
Children Eight, notably Arthur (1486-1502), Henry
VIII, Margaret (1489-1541) and Mary (1496-1533)

Gold sovereign of Henry VII, a
coin first struck in 1489 and
worth £1

Henry VII as a young man, 16th century drawing

Henry VII, terracotta bust by the Florentine sculptor Pietro Torrigiano c1508-9

Key facts Henry VII restored stable government and founded the Tudor Dynasty.

The last male Lancastrian claimant to the throne, Henry was exiled in Brittany during 1471-84 Yorkist rule. Then Yorkists split over Richard III's ill-founded claim to the crown. Heading a Lancastrian-Yorkist opposition, in 1485 Henry landed in Wales, defeated and killed Richard III at Bosworth, and became king. By marrying Elizabeth of York, he merged the houses of York and Lancaster, so ending the Wars of the Roses.

Henry crushed pretenders to the throne Lambert Simnel (1487) and Perkin Warbeck (1497), and boosted other classes at the expense of his troublesome nobles. He strengthened England's prestige and wealth by six commercial treaties and two marriage alliances. His son Arthur (and, after Arthur's death, Henry, later Henry VIII) was married to Catherine of Aragon (1501), and his daughter Margaret to King James IV of Scotland. In 1497 he backed the Italian Cabots' voyages from Bristol that stirred England's interest in North America. Henry was hard-headed, tough, and crafty, yet courteous, too, with an interest in learning. By his death he suffered from arthritis and gout.

HENRY VIII 1509-1547
Nicknames Bluff King Hal (posthumous), 'Father of the English Navy'
Authority King of England and Ireland (from

Coronation of Henry VIII and Queen Catherine (of Aragon) beneath their respective Tudor rose and pomegranate badges 1509, contemporary woodcut

1542), Calais and Boulogne (from 1544), Tournai (1513-19)
Dynasty House of Tudor
Parents Henry VII and Elizabeth of York, daughter of Edward IV, their second son
Born Greenwich Palace, Kent 28 June 1491
Succeeded to throne 22 Apr 1509
Crowned Westminster Abbey 24 June 1509
Reigned 37 years, 281 days
Died St James's Palace, London 28 Jan 1547
Buried St George's Chapel, Windsor Castle, Berks

Henry VIII medal
for his Supremacy
of the Church 1545

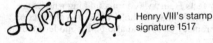

Henry VIII's stamp
signature 1517

Married (1) Catherine of Aragon (1485-1536),
daughter of King Ferdinand II of Spain, 11 June
1509 at Chapel of the Observant Friars; divorced
May 1533
(2) Anne Boleyn (1507-36), daughter of Sir
Thomas Boleyn, 25 Jan 1533 secretly at Whitehall
Palace ; beheaded for infidelity 19 May 1536
(3) Jane Seymour, daughter of Sir John Seymour,
30 May 1536 at Queen's Closet, Whitehall Palace;
died 24 Oct 1537
(4) Anne of Cleves (1515-57), second daughter of
John, Duke of Cleves, 6 Jan 1540 at Greenwich

Palace divorced July 1540

(5) Catherine Howard (c1520-42), daughter of
Lord Edmund Howard, 28 July 1540 at Oatlands
manor house, Surrey; beheaded for adultery 13
Feb 1542

(6) Catherine Parr (c1512-48), daughter of Sir
Thomas Parr, 12 July 1543 at Hampton Court
Palace

Children Henry, Prince of Wales (died aged two
months 1512), Mary (I) (by Catherine of Aragon),
Elizabeth I (by Anne Boleyn), Edward VI (by
Jane Seymour). Natural son Henry Fitzroy (by
mistress Elizabeth Blount) died 1536 aged about 20

Key facts Henry was a forceful king who broke
with the Roman Catholic Church by the Act of
Supremacy (1534) and also built a modern Royal
Navy.

Henry earned the still-held royal title 'Defender
of the Faith' from Pope Leo X in 1521 for his best-
selling book *The Defence of the Seven Sacraments*
rebutting the heresy of Martin Luther. Later he
established the Protestant Reformation in England
by creating the Church of England with the
monarch as supreme head. He suppressed
England's 823 monasteries, centralized
administrative authority, made use of Parliament's
powers, and left a modern fleet of 53 warships. In
1536 Henry incorporated Wales into England and
in 1542 made Ireland a kingdom. Henry waged
costly wars, leading victorious English troops at the
Battle of the Spurs or Guinegate, Artois, northern
France (1513), and spending heavily on later

Henry VIII in 1544 by Cornelis Massys

campaigns against France and Scotland (1542-6). He executed 50 alleged opponents. Henry's (successive) influential advisers were Thomas Wolsey, Thomas More, and Thomas Cromwell.

Henry was disloyal to wives and advisers, but remarriages partly reflected his aim to produce a male heir to keep the throne stable. Henry patronized the arts. A leg ulcer made his last years a misery.

EDWARD VI 1547-1553
Authority King of England and Ireland, Calais and Boulogne (till 1551)
Dynasty House of Tudor
Parents Henry VIII and Jane Seymour, their only child
Born Hampton Court Palace, Surrey 12 Oct 1537
Succeeded to the throne 28 Jan 1547
Crowned Westminster Abbey 19 Feb 1547
Reigned 6 years, 160 days
Died Greenwich Palace, Kent 6 July 1553
Buried Henry VII's Chapel, Westminster Abbey
Unmarried
Children None
Key facts Only nine on his accession, Edward was intellectually bright though obstinate, but died too young to shape government.

As Lord Protector, his uncle Edward Seymour, Duke of Somerset, chiefly controlled the nation's affairs until ousted in 1550 by the Regent John Dudley, Duke of Northumberland. A devout Protestant, Edward backed their aims to

Coronation medal of Edward VI 1547, the first such commemorative

consolidate the English Reformation. His reign produced the first *Book of Common Prayer* (1549) and the later-named Thirty-Nine Articles of Religion.

Dying of tuberculosis, Edward removed his half-sisters Mary and Elizabeth from the succession. And, under the Regent's influence, willed the crown to Northumberland's Protestant daughter-in-law Lady Jane Grey.

Jane the Quine

JANE 1553

Nickname The Nine Days Queen
Authority Queen of England and Ireland (only recognized by King's Lynn and Berwick)
Dynasty House of Grey
Parents Henry Grey, 3rd Marquess of Dorset, and Lady Frances Brandon (daughter of Henry VIII's younger sister Mary)
Born Bradgate Park, Leicestershire Sept 1537
Proclaimed queen 10 July 1553 (not crowned)
Reigned 9 days
Died Tower of London 12 Feb 1554
Buried Chapel of St Peter ad Vincula, the Tower
Married Lord Guildford Dudley (died 12 Feb 1554), fourth son of John Dudley, Duke of Northumberland, 21 May 1553 at Durham House, London
Children None
Key facts Jane was the beautiful and intelligent victim of a plot to usurp the throne.

In May 1553 she reluctantly married the fourth son of John Dudley, Duke of Northumberland, as part of the Duke's scheme to shift the royal succession from the Tudor to the Dudley family. Northumberland persuaded the dying Edward VI to settle the succession on Lady Jane and her male heirs. But nine days after Jane was declared queen, the Lord Mayor of London proclaimed Edward's sister Mary. Lacking widespread support, Jane and her husband were imprisoned and, after Wyatt's Rebellion, beheaded for treason.

MARY I 1553-1558
Nickname Bloody Mary
Authority Queen of England, Ireland and Calais
Dynasty House of Tudor
Parents Henry VIII and Catherine of Aragon, their only surviving child
Born Greenwich Palace, Kent 8 Feb 1516
Proclaimed queen 19 July 1553
Crowned Westminster Abbey 1 Oct 1553
Reigned 5 years, 122 days
Died St James's Palace, London 17 Nov 1558

Marriage medal of Philip and Mary 1554, by Jacopo da Trezzo of Milan

Buried Henry VII's Chapel, Westminster Abbey
Married Prince Philip II of Spain (1527-98), son of
Emperor Charles V, 25 July 1554 at Winchester
Cathedral (Philip was titled King of England but
without power)
Children None
Key facts A devout Roman Catholic and England's
first undisputed female sovereign, Mary ruthlessly
tried to suppress Protestantism in England.

She contracted an unpopular Spanish marriage
and repealed Edward VI's religious laws to re-
establish Roman Catholicism as the nation's only
creed. Mary became known as Bloody Mary for
burning 283 Protestant martyrs (1555-8) including
former Archbishop Thomas Cranmer. She joined
Spain in a war against France, losing Calais (7 Jan
1558), England's last toehold on mainland Europe.
Mary died of influenza, accepting that her
Protestant half-sister would succeed.

ELIZABETH I 1558-1603
Nicknames The Virgin Queen, Gloriana, Good
Queen Bess
Authority Queen of England, Ireland, and Virginia
(1587-91)
Dynasty House of Tudor
Parents Henry VIII and Anne Boleyn, their only
child
Born Greenwich Palace, Kent 7 Sept 1533
Succeeded to the throne 17 Nov 1558
Crowned Westminster Abbey 15 Jan 1559
Reigned 44 years, 127 days

Elizabeth I hawking 1575, from Tuberville's *Booke of Faulconrie*

Elizabeth I's
signature 1597

Died Richmond Palace, Surrey 24 Mar 1603
Buried Henry VII's Chapel, Westminster Abbey
Unmarried
Children None
Key facts Elizabeth proved an astute, cautious yet
forceful ruler commanding popular loyalty.

With the Act of Supremacy (1559) she re-
established the (Protestant) Church of England.
She survived Roman Catholic plots and eventually
executed her Catholic cousin and heir Mary,
Queen of Scots. Elizabeth finally fully supported
the Protestant Dutch Revolt against Spanish rule
(1585), and her ships defeated a Spanish invasion
fleet, the Invincible Armada (1588). Her reign saw
a dramatic upsurge in English literature, trade and
maritime activity, but the long Spanish war and
revolts in Ireland and England marred her last
years. She stayed single despite many royal suitors
and her attachment to Sir Robert Dudley (from
1564 the 1st Earl of Leicester of the 4th creation).
Elizabeth died of blood poisoning from a tonsillar
abscess.

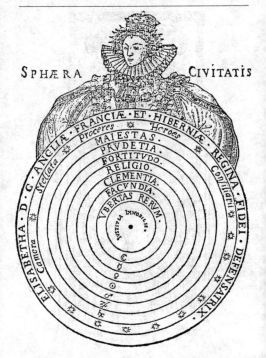

Elizabeth I's universe 1588, from John Case's *Sphaera Civitatis*

DIEV ET MON DROIT

James I in Parliament 1624

The House of Stuart
1603-1714

The Stuart family ruled Scotland from 1371 to 1603 and England and Scotland from 1603 to 1714. As sovereigns of England their name derives from Henry Stuart (Stewart) Lord Darnley and 4th Duke of Albany, cousin and second husband of Mary, Queen of Scots. Their son James VI of Scotland inherited England's throne (as James I) from his cousin Elizabeth I. Autocratic Stuart rule led to the English Civil Wars, but England and Scotland were formally united in 1707 as Great Britain under Queen Anne, the last Stuart ruler. The dynastic name became House of Stuart and Orange under William and Mary (1689-1694), and House of Orange during William's widowhood (1694-1702).

JAMES I (JAMES VI OF SCOTLAND) 1603-1625
Nicknames the British Solomon, 'the wisest fool in Christendom' (attrib to King Henry IV of France, r1598-1610)
Authority King of Great Britain, Ireland, Virginia (from 1607), New England (from 1620) and Bermuda (from 1609)
Dynasty House of Stuart
Parents Mary, Queen of Scots (Mary Stuart) and Henry Stuart, Lord Darnley, their only child

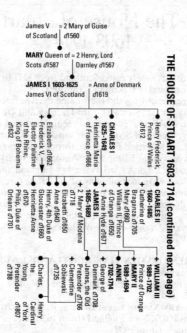

THE HOUSE OF STUART 1603-1714 (continued next page)

James V = 2 Mary of Guise
of Scotland   d1560

MARY Queen of = 2 Henry, Lord
Scots d1587   Darnley d1567

JAMES I 1603-1625 = Anne of Denmark
James VI of Scotland   d1619

+ Elizabeth d1662
+ Frederick V,
Elector Palatine
of the Rhine,
King of Bohemia
d1632

+ Charles I 1625-1649
+ Henrietta Maria
of France d1666

+ Henry Frederick,
Prince of Wales
d1612

+ Philip, Duke of
Orleans d1701

+ Henrietta Anne
d1670

+ Henry, 4th Duke of
Gloucester d1660

+ Anne d1640

+ Elizabeth d1650

+ Henry, 4th Duke of
Gloucester d1660

+ JAMES II 1685-1689
2 Mary of Modena
d1718
1 Anne Hyde d1671

+ Mary d1660

+ William II, Prince
of Orange d1650

+ Catherine of
Braganza d1705

+ CHARLES II
1660-1685

+ WILLIAM III
1689-1702
Prince of Orange

+ MARY II
1689-1694

+ ANNE
1702-1714

+ George of
Denmark d1708

James; the Old
Pretender d1766

2 Clementine
Sobieski
d1735

Charles,
the
Young
Pretender
d1788

Henry
Cardinal
of York
d1807

THE HOUSE OF STUART 1603-1714 (continued)

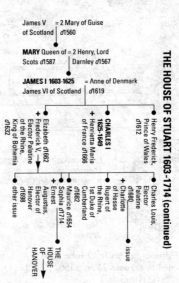

James V = 2 Mary of Guise
of Scotland d1560

MARY Queen of = 2 Henry, Lord
Scots d1587 Darnley d1567

JAMES I 1603-1625 = Anne of Denmark
James VI of Scotland d1619

+ Elizabeth d1662
Frederick V,
Elector Palatine
of the Rhine,
King of Bohemia
d1632

+ **CHARLES I**
1625-1649 = Henrietta Maria
of France d1666

Henry Frederick,
Prince of Wales
d1612

Charles Louis,
Elector
Palatine
d1680

+ Charlotte
of Hesse

Rupert of
the Rhine,
1st Duke of
Cumberland
d1682

+ Maurice d1654

+ Sophia d1714
Ernest
Augustus,
Elector of
Hanover

other issue
d1698

issue

THE
HOUSE
OF
HANOVER →

James I is warned of the Gunpowder Plot by Lord Monteagle's letter to his chief minister Robert Cecil, woodcut cartoon of 1617

Royal coat of arms, James I to James II

Born Edinburgh Castle 19 June 1566
Succeeded to thrones 24 July 1567 (Scotland); 24 Mar 1603 (England)
Crowned Church of the Holy Rood outside Stirling Castle 29 July 1567; Westminster Abbey 25 July 1603
Reigned 22 years, 3 days in England and 57 years, 246 days in Scotland
Died Theobalds Park, Hertfordshire 27 Mar 1625

James I welcomes home his son Prince Charles (l) from Madrid Oct 1623

James' signature as King of Scotland

Married Anne (1574-1619), daughter of King Frederick II of Denmark, 20 Aug 1590 at Oslo

Children Seven, notably Henry, Prince of Wales (1594-1612), Charles I, and Elizabeth (1596-1622)

Key facts James was a scholarly but autocratic ruler at odds with Parliament. King of Scotland on his mother's abdication, ruling through regents until 1583, he also became the first Stuart King of England and Ireland.

After ably asserting the crown in Scotland and

curbing factions, James stressed rule by divine right, but Parliament disputed his efforts to govern England as an absolute monarch. James supported the Anglican Church (Church of England). He persecuted the Protestant Puritans, and curbed Roman Catholic nobles' powers in Ireland and Scotland, giving Irish lands to Protestant Scots and English in the Plantation of Ulster (1611). James survived the (Catholic) Gunpowder Plot (1605). Abroad he sought peace at any price, executing courtier-navigator Sir Walter Raleigh for fighting in Spain's American colonies. The King James Bible translation (1611), commissioned by him, and North America's first permanent English colony, Jamestown (1607), were named in his honour. James wrote pedantic prose and verse. He died of kidney failure.

CHARLES I 1625-1649
Posthumous title Charles, King and Martyr
Authority King of Great Britain and Ireland, Virginia, New England, Maryland (from 1632), Nova Scotia (1628-32), Bermuda and five Caribbean islands
Dynasty House of Stuart
Parents James I (James VI of Scotland) and Anne, daughter of King Frederick II of Denmark, their second son and fourth child
Born Dunfermline Palace, Scotland 19 Nov 1600
Succeeded to throne 27 Mar 1625
Crowned Westminster Abbey 2 Feb 1626
Reigned 23 years, 319 days

Charles the Martyr, frontispiece of *Eikon Basilike* published on his burial day and reprinted 30 times in 1649, censorship notwithstanding

Died Whitehall, London 30 Jan 1649
Buried St George's Chapel, Windsor Castle, Berks
Married Henrietta Maria (1609-69), sister of King
Louis XIII of France, 1 May 1625 by proxy at
Notre Dame, Paris and 13 June at Canterbury
Cathedral
Children Nine, notably Charles II, Henrietta (1644-
70), Mary (1631-60), and James II
Key facts Charles was a reserved autocratic ruler
whose inflexibility led to civil war and his death.

Claiming rule by divine right, Charles clashed
with Parliament which rejected royal demands for
cash to wage costly wars. Charles three times
dissolved Parliament, ruling without it during
1629-40.

Then he tried seizing five dissident MPs, so
provoking the start of the English Civil Wars (1642-

Charles I's signature

Charles I in his Order of the Garter robes, 1649

Left: Charles I's execution

51). The Parliamentarians eventually crushed the Royalists at Marston Moor (1644) and Naseby (1645). Charles was later caught, convicted of treason, and beheaded in London.

Charles had been a sincerely religious king. He enjoyed hunting and patronized the arts.

CHARLES II 1660-1685

Nicknames Old Rowley, the Merry Monarch
Authority King of Great Britain and Ireland, ten American colonies, Bombay (1661-8), Tangier (1662-84), seven major Caribbean islands (Jamaica from 1655), Bermuda, Gold Coast
Dynasty House of Stuart

Bust of Charles II 1684, by Honoré Pellé

Charles II's signature c1669

Parents Charles I and Henrietta Maria, their eldest surviving son
Born St James's Palace, London 29 May 1630
Succeeded to throne 30 Jan 1649
Restored 29 May 1660
Crowned Westminster Abbey 23 Apr 1661
Reigned 36 years, 7 days
Died Whitehall Palace 6 Feb 1685
Buried Henry VII's Chapel, Westminster Abbey
Married Catherine of Braganza (1638-1705), daughter of John IV, Duke of Braganza and King of Portugal, 21 May 1662 at Portsmouth
Children James, Duke of Monmouth (1649-85) and 13 others, all illegitimate

The Restoration: Charles II re-enters the City of London

Key facts Charles was knowledgeable and witty, but pleasure-seeking and disloyal to his wife and ministers.

Exiled (1646) after defeat in the First English Civil War, he was proclaimed king (1649) but remained powerless while England was a Commonwealth and Protectorate (1649-59) dominated by Oliver Cromwell (Lord Protector 1653-8). Proclaimed King of the Scots (1651), Charles invaded England but fled to France after losing the Battle of Worcester (1651). Recalled by Parliament, Charles effectively began reigning in 1660, with wide powers.

The Restoration saw profligate spending on Court pleasures, a revival of drama (suppressed under Commonwealth rule), and the founding of the Royal Society. Charles played off ministers against one another and survived the Rye House murder plot (1683). But the Great Plague (1665), Fire of London (1666) and two costly sea wars with the Dutch marred his reign, and he conceded some loss of royal power. After a last-minute conversion to Roman Catholicism he died of uraemia and mercury poisoning.

JAMES II (JAMES VII OF SCOTLAND) 1685-1688
Authority King of Great Britain and Ireland, eleven American colonies, seven major Caribbean islands, Bermuda
Dynasty House of Stuart
Parents Charles I and Henrietta Maria, their second son

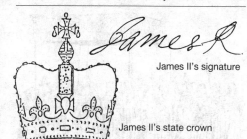

James II's signature

James II's state crown

Born St James's Palace, London 14 Oct 1633
Succeeded to throne 6 Feb 1685
Crowned Westminster Abbey 23 Apr 1685
Reigned 3 years, 309 days
Died Château of Saint Germain-en-Laye, near Versailles 6 Sept 1701
Buried Saint Germain parish church and Church of the English Benedictines, Paris
Married (1) Anne Hyde (1637-71), eldest daughter of Edward Hyde, Lord Chancellor and 1st Earl of Clarendon, 3 Sept 1660 at Worcester House, The Strand, London and (2) Mary of Modena (Maria Beatrice d' Este), only daughter of Alfonso IV, Duke of Modena, 30 Sept 1673 by proxy at Modena, then 21 Nov at Dover
Children 15, notably Mary II and Anne by Anne Hyde, and James (the Old Pretender) by Mary
Key facts James was a libertine noted for personal bravery and pro-Catholic reforms provoking Protestant hostility that lost him the throne.

James II's coronation procession

As Lord High Admiral (1660-73 and 1684-8), he strengthened the Royal Navy and led it in two battles against Dutch fleets, but lost popularity by his 1668 conversion to Catholicism. As King, by favouring Roman Catholic appointments in the Church, Law and Army, James aroused popular fears of a Catholic tyranny, reinforced by the birth of his son (the future Old Pretender, recognized by Jacobites as James III of England and James VIII of Scotland) in 1688.

James's opponents sparked off the Glorious Revolution by inviting Protestant William II of Orange, who arrived with an invasion force. Defections by the royal army forced James to flee to France. Parliament declared James had abdicated (12 Feb 1689) and William and Mary

James II and Queen Mary (of Modena) coronation
medal, by George Bower

accepted the throne. James landed in Ireland in
March 1689 but William defeated his Irish-French
army at the Boyne (1/12 July 1690). James returned
to France and later died of a stroke.

WILLIAM III 1689-1702
Nickname King Billy (posthumous Irish Protestant
salutation)
Authority King of England, Scotland and Ireland
(respectively as William III, II and I), reigning
jointly with (*see*) Mary II. Stadholder of the
Netherlands (since 24 June 1672). Also recognized
by eleven American colonies, seven major
Caribbean islands, Bermuda, and Dutch overseas
possessions

Royal coat of arms, William III (Lion of Nassau added)

Commemorative medal to William III, 1705

Dynasty House of Stuart and Orange
Parents Mary (daughter of Charles I) and Stadholder William II, 4th Prince of Orange-Nassau (reigned 1647-50)
Born The Hague, Holland 4 Nov 1650
Proclaimed king 13 Feb 1689
Reigned 13 years, 23 days
Crowned Westminster Abbey 11 Apr 1689
Died Kensington Palace, London 8 Mar 1702
Married Mary, William's cousin and eldest daughter of the Duke of York, later James II, 4 Nov 1677 at St James's Palace, London
Key facts William and Mary accepted a Bill of Rights curbing royal power and restricting succession to the throne to Protestants. They ruled jointly until Mary's death.

As 5th Prince of Orange-Nassau and Stadholder of five of the United Provinces of the Netherlands (from 1672), Dutch-raised Protestant William led

the last-ditch but successful Dutch defence against
Louis XIV's French invasion. In England's
Glorious Revolution of 1688 he ousted James II by
landing Dutch troops at Torbay at the invitation of
James's opponents, later crushing Irish and
Scottish resistance. He then fought Louis XIV to a
stalemate on the Continent by 1697 in the Nine
Years War; until 1693 his allies included the Pope.

William proved an able coalition diplomat and
conscientious administrator but a reserved and
unpopular monarch. He died of pneumonia after a
fall from his horse.

MARY II 1689–1694
Authority Queen of England, Scotland and Ireland
Dynasty House of Stuart
Parents Duke of York (later James II) and Anne
Hyde, their elder surviving daughter
Born St James's Palace, London 30 Apr 1662
Proclaimed queen 13 Feb 1689
Crowned Westminster Abbey 11 Apr 1689
Reigned 4 years, 319 days
Died Kensington Palace, London 28 Dec 1694
Buried Henry VII's Chapel, Westminster Abbey
Married Prince William of Orange, a cousin, 4 Nov
1677 at St James's Palace, London
Children None
Key facts Mary was a popular princess in Holland.
After the Glorious Revolution she joined William
in England, becoming joint sovereign.

Mary administered government while William
was abroad but acted upon his advice. Mary's

William and Mary's coronation from a 1689
Protestant ballad sheet

Mary II's signature
1689-94

Dutch tastes helped influence English domestic
design, and her selfless good nature won much
respect. She died of smallpox.

ANNE 1702-1714
Dynasty House of Stuart
Authority Queen of Great Britain and Ireland,
twelve American colonies, seven major Caribbean
islands, Gibraltar (from 1704), Minorca (from
1708), Nova Scotia (from 1710), New Brunswick
(from 1713)

Anne's signature

Royal coat of arms, Anne

Parents Duke of York (later James II) and Anne Hyde, their second daughter
Born St James's Palace, London 6 Feb 1665
Succeeded to throne 8 Mar 1702
Crowned Westminster Abbey 23 Apr 1702
Reigned 12 years, 146 days
Died Kensington Palace, London 1 Aug 1714
Buried Henry VII's Chapel, Westminster Abbey
Married Prince George of Denmark (1653-1708), second son of King Frederick III of Denmark, 28 July 1683 at Chapel Royal, St James's Palace
Children None surviving her, but 17 including miscarriages
Key facts Anne supported the Church of England and presided over Cabinet meetings, remaining mainly above the new political parties called Whigs and Tories. In 1707 she saw a single parliament created for England and Scotland by the Act of Union.

Anne was religious and noted for homely virtues, but lacked broader interests. The outstanding achievements in the War of the

Second Great Seal of Anne
1707, for the Act of Union
between England and Scotland

Spanish Succession (1702-13) were the work of her
Captain-General, John Churchill, 1st Duke of
Marlborough, whose wife Sarah was Anne's oldest
friend (until 1710). Her many pregnancies
produced only one child who survived infancy
William Henry, Duke of Gloucester (1689-1700)
and her husband died in 1708. Anne's death from a
stroke ended Stuart rule.

The House of Hanover
1714-1901

This dynasty of German origin takes its name from George I's father Ernest Augustus, 1st Elector of Hanover in north-west Germany (Electors were princes of the Holy Roman Empire who elected the emperor). George I inherited the British crown through his mother Sophia, a Protestant granddaughter of James I. The Hanoverian sovereigns lost influence to Parliament but presided over a nation that became the leading world power under the last Hanoverian monarch, Queen Victoria.

Royal coat of arms, George I to III (till 1801) with the white horse of Hanover

George I's signature

GEORGE I 1702-1714
Authority King of Great Britain and Ireland, twelve American colonies, seven major Caribbean islands, Gibraltar, Minorca, New Brunswick; 2nd

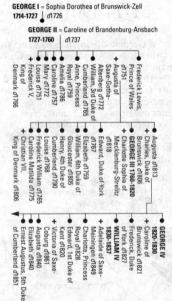

THE HOUSE OF HANOVER 1714-1901 (continued next page)

GEORGE I = Sophia Dorothea of Brunswick-Zell
1714-1727   d1726

GEORGE II = Caroline of Brandenburg-Ansbach
1727-1760   d1737

+ Frederick Lewis, Prince of Wales d1751
+ Augusta of Saxe-Gotha-Altenberg d1772
William, 3rd Duke of Cumberland d1765
Anne, Princess Royal d1759
Amelia d1786
Caroline d1757
Mary d1772
+ Louisa d1751
+ Frederick V, King of Denmark d1766

+ Augusta of Brunswick d1813
+ Charles, Duke of Brunswick d1806
+ GEORGE III **1760-1820**
+ Charlotte Sophia of Mecklenburg-Strelitz d1818
Edward, Duke of York d1767
Elizabeth d1759
William, 6th Duke of Gloucester d1805
Henry, 4th Duke of Cumberland d1790
Louisa d1768
+ Frederick William d1765
+ Caroline Matilda d1775
+ Christian VII, King of Denmark d1806

GEORGE IV
1820-1830
+ Caroline of Brunswick d1821
Frederick, Duke of York d1827
WILLIAM IV **1830-1837**
+ Adelaide of Saxe-Meiningen d1849
Charlotte, Princess Royal d1828
Edward, 1st Duke of Kent d1820
+ Victoria of Saxe-Coburg d1861
Augusta d1840
Elizabeth d1840
Ernest Augustus, 5th Duke of Cumberland d1851

THE HOUSE OF HANOVER 1714-1901 (continued)

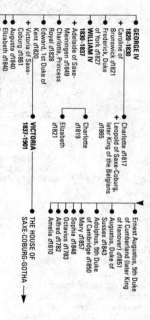

GEORGE IV
1820-1830
+ Caroline of
Brunswick d1821
Frederick, Duke
of York d1827

WILLIAM IV
1830-1837
+ Adelaide of Saxe-
Meiningen d1849
Charlotte, Princess
Royal d1828
Edward, 1st Duke of
Kent d1820
+ Victoria of Saxe-
Coburg d1861
Augusta d1840
Elizabeth d1840
Ernest Augustus, 5th Duke
of Cumberland d1851

Charlotte d1817
+ Leopold of Saxe-Coburg,
later King of the Belgians
d1865

Charlotte
d1819
Elizabeth
d1821

VICTORIA
1837-1901
+ Victoria of Saxe-

Ernest Augustus, 5th Duke
of Cumberland (later King
of Hanover) d1851
Augustus, Duke of
Sussex d1843
Adolphus, 5th Duke
of Cambridge d1850
Mary d1857
Sophia d1848
Octavius d1783
Alfred d1782
Amelia d1810

THE HOUSE OF
SAXE-COBURG-GOTHA →

A Jacobite conspiracy
confounded 1722/3

A very rare medal of
George I's proclamation
as King 12 Aug 1714

Elector of Hanover (since 1698)
Dynasty House of Hanover
Parents Ernest Augustus (1629-98), 1st Elector of
Hanover (1692-8), and Princess Sophia (1630-
1714),a granddaughter of James I, their eldest son
Born Osnabrück, Hanover 28 May 1660
Succeeded to throne 1 Aug 1714
Crowned Westminster Abbey 20 Oct 1714
Reigned 12 years, 314 days
Died Osnabrück, Hanover 11 June 1727
Buried Leineschlosskirche, Hanover; reburied

Herrenhausen Palace during Second World War
Married Sophia Dorothea of Celle (1666-1726), a
cousin and only daughter of George William, Duke
of Lüneburg-Celle, 21 Nov 1682 (divorced 1694)
Children George II and Sophia Dorothea
Key facts George spoke only German and French
when he came to the throne at 54 under the 1701
Act of Settlement conferring the succession on his
mother and her Protestant heirs.

Early on he survived a Scottish pro-Stuart revolt
(The First Jacobite Rebellion 1715). George
appointed a Whig ministry and came to depend
upon his powerful ministers Sir Robert Walpole
and Viscount Charles Townshend. He kept in close
touch with his German possessions and died of a
stroke on a visit to Hanover.

George was a capable military leader and a
patron of Handel but an unpopular autocrat,
widely disliked for his rapacious and ugly
mistresses and for imprisoning his wife for life.

GEORGE II 1727-1760
Authority King of Great Britain and Ireland,
thirteen American colonies (from 1732), Gibraltar,
Minorca (till 1756), West Indies (part), Canada
(from 1759), Indian possessions (especially Bengal
from 1757); 3rd Elector of Hanover
Dynasty House of Hanover
Parents Crown Prince George of Hanover (later
George I) and Sophia Dorothea of Celle, their
only son
Born Herrenhausen Palace, Hanover 30 Oct 1683

George II's signature

Accession medal of George II, by E Hannibal

Succeeded to throne 11 June 1727
Crowned Westminster Abbey 11 Oct 1727
Reigned 33 years, 136 days
Died Westminster Palace, London 25 Oct 1760
Buried Henry VII's Chapel, Westminster Abbey
Married Caroline of Ansbach (1683-1737), daughter of John Frederick, Margrave of Brandenburg-Ansbach 22 Aug 1705 at Hanover
Children Three sons and five daughters, notably Frederick, Prince of Wales (1707-51), Anne (1709-59), William, Duke of Cumberland (1721-65), Mary (1723-72), and Louisa (1724-51)

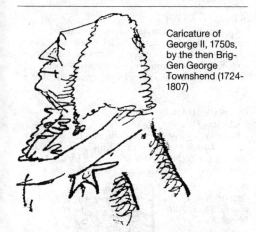

Caricature of George II, 1750s, by the then Brig-Gen George Townshend (1724-1807)

Key facts A brave soldier, at the victory of Dettingen (1743) George became the last British king to lead troops in battle. Politically he was influenced by ministers, notably Sir Robert Walpole and William Pitt the Elder. This hastened the trend toward constitutional monarchy.

George's reign saw major agricultural and manufacturing advances heralding great social and political change. His Hanoverian rule survived a Stuart revolt (the Second Jacobite Rebellion 1745-6) suppressed by his son William; and unprecedented overseas victories in the Seven Years' War (1756-63) began building British power in Canada and India.

George was methodical, stubborn and detail-obsessed, but often deftly guided by the formidable Queen Caroline in matters of state. Like his father, his interests were military, extra-marital and musical: he too was Handel's patron. He died of a heart attack.

GEORGE III 1760-1820
Nickname Farmer George
Authority King of Great Britain and Ireland; from 1 Jan 1801 King of the United Kingdom of Great Britain and Ireland. Also recognized by the thirteen American colonies (until 1776); West

Royal coat of arms 1801-16 (below) and 1816 to William IV (right)

George III's signature 1782

George III's Gold State Coach built 1762 and used for
all coronations since 1820

Indies (most); Canada; Sierra Leone (from 1787);
Gambia (resettled 1816); New South Wales (from
1788); India (parts); Ceylon and other islands(from
1795); Malacca (1795-1818); Singapore (1819); Java
(1811-18); Cape Colony (from 1806); Gibraltar;
Corsica (1794-6); Malta (from 1800); Ionian Islands
(from 1814); Minorca (1763-81, 1798-1802); 4th
Elector of Hanover (*de facto* till 1803), King of
Hanover (1814)
Parents Frederick Louis, Prince of Wales and
Princess Augusta of Saxe-Coburg-Gotha (1719-72)
Born Norfolk House, St James's Square, London 4
June 1738
Succeeded to throne 25 Oct 1760

George III and Queen Charlotte watch Napoleon's invasion attempt, Gillray cartoon 1804

Crowned Westminster Abbey 22 Sept 1761
Reigned 59 years, 96 days
Died Windsor Castle, Berks 29 Jan 1820
Married Charlotte Sophia of Mecklenburg-Strelitz

(1744-1818), youngest daughter of Charles Louis, Frederick, Duke of Mecklenburg-Strelitz 8 Sept 1761 at St James's Palace
Children 15, notably George IV, Frederick, Duke of York (1763-1827), William IV, Edward (1767-1825), Ernest (1771-1851), Augustus (1773-1843) and Adolphus (1774-1850)
Key facts His immensely long reign saw dramatic national changes. Britain's population doubled, the Industrial Revolution accelerated, new social classes arose, and modern party politics began taking shape. Abroad, Britain lost all her American colonies (1783) and endured a prolonged but victorious war with Revolutionary and Napoleonic France (1793-1815).The 1801 Act of Union cemented Ireland's ties with Great Britain and before George's death Britain was Europe's chief power, with a growing world empire.

The most productive begetter of legitimate children since Edward III, George proved hardworking, far more British and cultivated in outlook than his Hanoverian forebears. He was the first George to show interest in the Royal Navy and virtually recreated the Royal Library. He chose the long-serving prime ministers Lord North (1770-82) and William Pitt the Younger (1784-1801, 1804-6).

People blamed George for losing the American colonies, and in 1765 he suffered the first of several increasingly severe attacks of apparent insanity, due to the rare and incurable ailment porphyria. Domestic virtues and good humour later earned him much popular affection. His eldest son Prince George became regent on 5 February 1811. Deaf and blind, George III is said to have died of senility.

GEORGE IV 1820-1830
Nickname Prinny
Authority King of the United Kingdom of Great Britain and Ireland, Canada, four Australian colonies, West Indies (most), India (parts), Ceylon and other islands, Malta, Gibraltar, Ionian Islands, four West African and two South African colonies; King of Hanover
Dynasty House of Hanover
Parents George III and Charlotte Sophia, their eldest son
Born St James's Palace, London 12 Aug 1762
Succeeded to throne 29 Jan 1820
Crowned Westminster Abbey 19 July 1821
Reigned 10 years, 148 days
Died Windsor Castle, Berks 26 June 1830
Buried St George's Chapel, Windsor Castle, Berks
Married (1) (secretly, later annulled) Mrs Maria Fitzherbert, née Smythe and a Catholic (1756-1837), 15 Dec 1785 at Park Street, Mayfair, London; and (2) Caroline (1768-1821), his first cousin and second daughter of Charles, Duke of Brunswick (1735-1806), 8 Apr 1795 at the Chapel Royal, St James's Palace, London
Children Charlotte (by Caroline), died in childbirth (1817)
Key facts As Prince Regent (1811-20) then King,

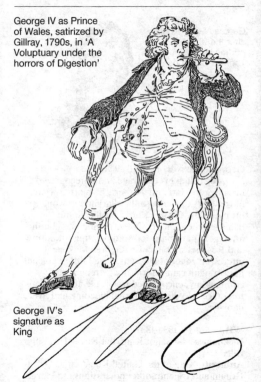

George IV as Prince of Wales, satirized by Gillray, 1790s, in 'A Voluptuary under the horrors of Digestion'

George IV's signature as King

George IV, engraving
after the 1818
portrait by Sir
Thomas Lawrence

George effectively reigned 19 years.

Disregarding his underage and unrecognized
marriage to Maria Fitzherbert, he married (later
ill-treating) Caroline so that Parliament would pay
off his debts. George's lazy, profligate life
damaged the monarchy's moral influence, but his
intelligent patronage fostered painting, literature,
and Regency architecture. George took small
interest in government, and played little personal
part in significant reforms that strengthened
criminal law, encouraged free trade and religious
tolerance. He died of internal bleeding and liver
damage.

WILLIAM IV 1830-1837
Nicknames The Sailor King, the Royal Tar, Silly
Billy
Authority King of the United Kingdom of Great
Britain and Ireland; other possessions as George

Great Seal of
William IV

IV plus South Australia (1836); King of Hanover
Dynasty House of Hanover
Parents George III and Charlotte Sophia of
Mecklenburg-Strelitz, their third son
Born Buckingham Palace 21 Aug 1765
Succeeded to throne 26 June 1830
Crowned Westminster Abbey 8 Sept 1831
Reigned 6 years, 359 days
Died Windsor Castle, Berks 20 June 1837
Buried St George's Chapel, Windsor Castle, Berks
Married Princess Adelaide of Saxe-Meiningen
(1792-1849), eldest daughter of George, 6th Duke
of Saxe-Meiningen, 11 July 1818 at Kew, Surrey
Children Two daughters who died in infancy and 10
illegitimate children by actress Mrs Dorothea
Jordan (1762-1816)
Key facts William was nearly 65 when he inherited

William IV contemplates his reign's key issue 1832

the throne from his brother George IV.

William had fought in the Royal Navy during the American Revolution. Later as Duke of Clarence (from 1789) he won a reputation for womanizing but took government affairs more seriously than George. William reluctantly helped to push through the 1832 Reform Act that began shifting power from the sovereign and aristocracy to the industrialized masses. He died of pneumonia and liver failure.

VICTORIA 1837-1901

Nickname Grandmother of Europe (due to her children's royal marriages)

Authority Queen of the United Kingdom of Great Britain and Ireland, and (from 1 May 1876) Empress of India; 28 major colonies annexed or leased in Africa and Asia from New Zealand (1840) to Transvaal (1900)

Dynasty House of Hanover

Parents Edward, 1st Duke of Kent, George III's fourth son (1767-1820), and Victoria of Saxe-Coburg (1786-1861), widow of Prince Emich of Leiningen and daughter of Francis, Duke of Saxe-Coburg-Saalfeld

Born Kensington Palace, London 24 May 1819

Succeeded to throne 20 June 1837

Crowned Westminster Abbey 28 June 1838

Reigned 63 years 216 days

Died Osborne, Isle of Wight, 22 Jan 1901

Buried Frogmore, Windsor Home Park, Berks

Married Prince Albert of Saxe-Coburg-Gotha (1819-61), a first cousin and son of Ernest I, 1st Duke of Saxe-Coburg-Gotha, 10 Feb 1840 at St James's Palace, London

Children Victoria (1840-1901), Albert (Edward VII), Alice (1843-78), Alfred (1844-1900), Helena (1846-1923), Louise (1848-1939), Arthur (1850-1942), Leopold (1853-84), and Beatrice (1857-1944)

Key facts Britain's longest-reigning monarch, Victoria set high moral standards and restored the monarchy's dignity. The monarchy lost power but became the ceremonial symbol of British imperial

Victoria on the 1840 Penny Black, the first royal postage stamp

Royal coat of arms, Victoria to the present

might which reached its climax in her reign.

Inheriting the throne aged only 18, she learned statecraft from Prime Minister Lord Melbourne and later from Albert, her husband whom she made Prince Consort in 1857. His keen interests in music, painting, and science influenced hers, and his early death (1861) deeply distressed her. From then on Victoria wore black and lived in seclusion, largely at Balmoral in Scotland and Osborne in the Isle of Wight. But she remained politically aware, often receiving successive prime ministers, notably William Gladstone and Benjamin Disraeli. She died after a brief, painless illness.

Victoria lived to reign over an empire containing one quarter of all land and people on Earth. Its trade and industrial drive made Victorian Britain the world's richest nation, with a broadening democracy and increasing range of social reforms.

Victoria's signature

Victoria soon
after her
accession

Victoria in her Golden Jubilee year 1897, woodcut by
Sir William Nicholson

The House of Saxe-Coburg-Gotha, later Windsor (1901-   )

The present royal house originated in the Saxe-Coburg line of the Ernestine Wettins, the old European dynasty that produced Queen Victoria's German husband Prince Albert. Their son Edward VII and his son George V were Wettins, but George assumed the name Windsor in 1917 to sever the British royal family's links with a then hostile Germany. The Windsors have played a symbolic role as national figureheads. Although Queen Elizabeth II married Philip Mountbatten, by proclamation their male-line descendants with a royal title will be known as members of the House of Windsor; other descendants will be called Mountbatten-Windsor.

EDWARD VII 1901-1910
Nicknames the Peacemaker, Tum-tum
Authority King of the United Kingdom of Great Britain and Ireland and British Dominions overseas; Emperor of India
Dynasty House of Saxe-Coburg-Gotha
Parents Queen Victoria and Prince Albert of Saxe-Coburg-Gotha, their eldest son
Born Buckingham Palace, London 9 Nov 1841
Succeeded to the throne 22 Jan 1901

THE HOUSE OF SAXE-COBURG-GOTHA 1901-1917

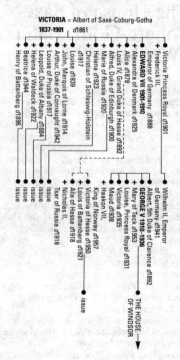

VICTORIA = Albert of Saxe-Coburg-Gotha
1837-1901   d1861

+ Victoria Princess Royal d1901
  + Frederick III
  + Wilhelm II, Emperor of Germany d1941

+ EDWARD VII 1901-1910
  + Alexandra of Denmark d1925
  + Albert 5th Duke of Clarence d1892
  + Louise, Princess Royal d1931
  + GEORGE V 1910-1936
    + Mary of Teck d1953
  + Victoria d1935
  + Maud d1938
    + Haakon VII, King of Norway d1957

+ Alice d1878
  + Louis IV, Grand Duke of Hesse d1892
  + Victoria of Hesse d1950
    + Louis of Battenberg d1921
  + Alix of Hesse d1918
    + Nicholas II, Tsar of Russia d1918

+ Alfred, Duke of Edinburgh d1900
  + Marie of Russia d1920

+ Helena d1923
  + Christian of Schleswig-Holstein d1917

+ Louise d1939
  + John, Marquis of Lorne d1914

+ Arthur, Duke of Connaught d1942

+ Leopold, Duke of Albany d1884
  + Helena of Waldeck d1922

+ Beatrice d1944
  + Henry of Battenberg d1896

+ Louise of Prussia d1917

issue
issue
issue
issue
issue
issue
issue
issue

THE HOUSE OF WINDSOR →

CORONATION OF
THEIR MAJESTIES
KING EDWARD VII
AND
QVEEN ALEXANDRA

BY COMMAND OF THE KING THE EARL MARSHAL
IS DIRECTED TO INVITE

TO

BE PRESENT AT THE ABBEY CHVRCH OF WESTMINSTER
ON THE 26ᵗʰ DAY OF IVNE 1902

EARL MARSHAL

Coronation invitation with the original date. Edward's illness forced a postponement

Crowned Westminster Abbey 9 Aug 1902
Reigned 9 years, 199 days
Died Buckingham Palace, London 6 May 1910
Buried St George's Chapel, Windsor Castle, Berks
Married Princess Alexandra of Denmark (1844-1925), daughter of King Christian IX of Denmark, 10 Mar 1863 at St George's Chapel, Windsor Castle

Edward VII's signature

Order of Merit (Badge, Civil Division) founded by Edward VII 23 June 1902

Children Six including Edward (1864-92), George V, Louise (1867-1931), Victoria (1868-1935), and Maude (1869-1938)

Key facts Aged 59 when he ascended the throne, (Albert) Edward proved an affable, popular king, adding diplomacy to his established roles of princely sportsman and socialite.

Early irresponsibilities had incurred his mother's lifelong disapproval, and his free-and-easy social activities gave rise to scandals. Created Prince of Wales (1841), he was excluded from public service by Victoria and gained a reputation for enjoying women's company (13 known mistresses), gambling, horse-racing, shooting, the theatre, yachting, and travel in Europe.

On becoming King, Edward revived the monarchy's splendour, which had lapsed during Victoria's years of seclusion. He was politically aware, and worked to reinforce Britain's position in Europe and to prevent a new major war. He strengthened Anglo-French and Anglo-Russian relations, but failed to make friends with his nephew Kaiser Wilhelm II of Germany and aroused German suspicions of a British plan to surround Germany with a hostile alliance. Edward died of bronchitis.

Munich cartoon of Prince Edward's legendary
socializing 1901

THE HOUSE OF WINDSOR 1917- (continued next page)

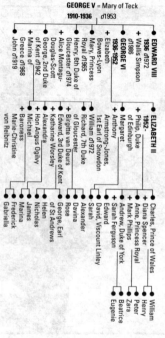

GEORGE V = Mary of Teck
1910-1936 *d*1953

- **EDWARD VIII**
  1936 *d*1972
  + Wallis Simpson
  *d*1986

- **GEORGE VI**
  1936-1952
  + Elizabeth
  Bowes-Lyon

- Mary, Princess
  Royal *d*1965

- Henry, 6th Duke of
  Gloucester *d*1974
  + Alice Montagu-
  Douglas-Scott

- George, 2nd Duke
  of Kent *d*1942
  + Marina of
  Greece *d*1968

- **ELIZABETH II**
  1952-
  + Philip, Duke
  of Edinburgh

- Margaret
  + Anthony
  Armstrong-Jones,
  1st Earl of Snowdon

- William *d*1972

- Richard, 7th Duke
  of Gloucester
  + Birgitte van Deurs

- Edward, 3rd Duke of Kent
  + Katharine Worsley

- Alexandra
  + Hon Angus Ogilvy

- Michael
  + Baroness
  Marie-Christine
  von Reibnitz

- John *d*1919

- Charles, Prince of Wales
  + Diana Spencer

- Anne, Princess Royal
  + Mark Phillips

- Andrew, Duke of York
  + Sarah Ferguson

- Edward

- George, Earl
  of St Andrews

- Helen

- Nicholas

- James

- Marina

- David, Viscount Linley

- Sarah

- Alexander

- Davina

- Rose

- William

- Henry

- Peter

- Zara

- Beatrice

- Eugenie

- Frederick

- Gabriella

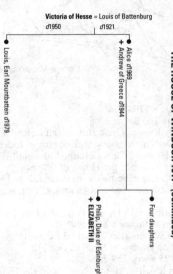

THE HOUSE OF WINDSOR 1917- (continued)

Victoria of Hesse = Louis of Battenberg
d1950   d1921

Louis, Earl Mountbatten d1979

Alice d1969
+ Andrew of Greece d1944

Philip, Duke of Edinburgh
+ ELIZABETH II

Four daughters

George V's signature as
King-Emperor

GEORGE V 1910-1936
Nickname The Sailor King
Authority King of Great Britain and Ireland and
British Dominions overseas; Emperor of India
Dynasty House of Saxe-Coburg-Gotha until 17 July
1917 when renamed the House of Windsor
Parents Prince Albert Edward (later Edward VII)
and Princess Alexandra of Denmark, their second
son
Born Marlborough House, London 3 June 1865
Succeeded to throne 6 May 1910
Crowned Westminster Abbey 22 June 1911;
Coronation Durbar at Delhi 12 Dec 1911
Reigned 25 years, 259 days
Died Sandringham House, Norfolk 20 Jan 1936
Buried St George's Chapel, Windsor Castle
Married Princess Mary of Teck (1867-1953), only
daughter of Francis, Duke of Teck 6 July 1893 at St
James's Palace, London
Children Edward VIII, George (George VI), Mary
(1897-1965), Henry (1900-74), George Edward
(1902-42) and John (1905-19)

George V as
Captain of the new
cruiser HMS
Crescent 1892

The British Empire was at its largest in 1920 under
George V after conquests in the Great War

• Islands/small territories

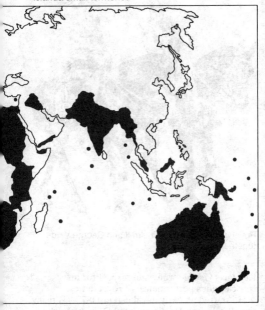

Royal cousins Kaiser Wilhelm II and George V ride together before 1914

Key facts George won wide respect for his conscientious performance of royal duties.

He started an early naval career (1877-93) rising to vice-admiral. He was created Duke of York in 1892. While still Prince of Wales, between 1901 and 1908 he represented Edward VII in visits to

Britain's overseas empire, and in 1911 revisited India for his own imperial coronation.

When Britain fought Germany in World War I George regularly visited the Western Front as well as munitions factories and changed the British royal family's name from the German Saxe-Coburg-Gotha to the English Windsor. George at times played an influential role in British politics. He contributed to a settlement creating the Irish Free State (1921); chose Stanley Baldwin as Conservative prime minister (1923); and in the 1931 financial crisis persuaded Labour, Conservative, and Liberal parties to form a national coalition government. He made the first Christmas broadcast (1932). George enjoyed shooting game and he built a world-famous collection of postage stamps. In later life he suffered ill-health; he died of bronchitis.

EDWARD VIII 1936
Nickname Our Smiling Prince
Authority King of Great Britain and Ireland and British Dominions overseas; Emperor of India
Dynasty House of Windsor
Parents George, Duke of York (later George V) and Princess Mary of Teck (later Queen Mary), their eldest son
Born White Lodge, Richmond Park, Surrey 23 June 1894
Succeeded to throne 20 Jan 1936
Reigned 325 days (uncrowned)
Abdicated 10 Dec 1936

Edward as Prince of Wales and Colonel of the Welsh Guards, 1932

Died Paris 28 May 1972
Buried Frogmore House, Windsor Home Park, Berks
Married Mrs Wallis Simpson (1896-1986) 3 June 1937 at Château Condé, Monts, near Tours, France
Children None
Key facts King Edward VIII is best remembered for abdicating rather than abandon plans to marry American divorcee Mrs Wallis Warfield Simpson.

He was educated at the Royal Naval College and

LATE NEWS!

The Evening News

Yeast-Vite

LARGEST EVENING NET SALE IN THE WORLD

BROADCASTING PAGE 9

LATE EXTRA

ONE PENNY

THE KING ABDICATES

'My Final and Irrevocable Decision": The Duke of York Succeeds To The Throne at Once

'I CAN NO LONGER DISCHARGE MY HEAVY TASK WITH EFFICIENCY"

Abdication Instrument Signed To-day With The Three Royal Brothers as Witnesses

MESSAGE READ TO PARLIAMENT

"My Mind Is Made Up : Further Delay Cannot But Be Most Injurious"

King Edward the Eighth has abdicated his Throne. He announced his decision in the following message which he sent to Parliament this afternoon and which was read by the Speaker to the House of Commons:

After long and anxious consideration, I have determined to renounce the Throne to which I succeeded on the death of my Father, and I am now communicating this My final and irrevocable decision.

Realising as I do the gravity of this step, I can only hope that I shall have the understanding of My peoples in the decision I have taken and the reasons which have led me to take it.

I will not enter now into My private feelings, but I would beg that it should be remembered that the burden which constantly rests upon the shoulders of a Sovereign is so heavy that it can only be borne in circumstances different from those in which I now find Myself.

I concieve that I am not overlooking the duty that rests on Me to place in the forefront the public interest, when I declare that I am conscious that I can no longer discharge this heavy task with efficiency or with satisfaction to Myself.

THE ABDICATION INSTRUMENT

I have therefore this morning executed an Instrument of Abdication in the terms following :

"I, Edward the VIII of Gt. Britain, Ireland and the Dominions beyond the Seas, King, Emperor of India, do hereby declare my irrevocable determination to renounce the Throne for Myself and for my descendants, and My desire that effect should be given to this Instrument of Abdication immediately

"In taken whereof I have hereunto set My hand this twelth day of December, nineteen hundred and thirty-six, in the presence of the witnesses whose signatures are subscribed

(Signed) Edward R."

My execution of this Instrument has been witnessed by My three brothers, Their Royal Highnesses The Duke of York, the Duke of Gloucester and the Duke of Kent.

I deeply appreciate the spirit which has actuated the appeals which have been made to Me to take a different decision, and I have before reaching my final determination most fully pondered upon it.

But my mind is made up. Moreover, further delay cannot but be most injurious to the peoples whom I have served as Prince of Wales and as King and whose future happiness and prosperity are the constant aim of My heart.

I take My leave of them in the confident hope that the course which I have thought it right to follow is that which is best for the stability of the Throne and Empire, and the happiness of My peoples.

"NO DELAY OF ANY KIND"

The King To Go Abroad

New King May Be George VI

Proclamation on Saturday

Sensational Speech By Mr. Baldwin

"THE KING SAID : 'I AM GOING TO MARRY MRS. SIMPSON. . . I AM PREPARED TO GO' "

Before The Cabinet

He Must Settle It"

"I Am Prepared To Go"

A Painful Task

This Night Of History

Oxford University, created Prince of Wales in 1911, and served in World War I. Good looks, charm, diplomacy, and democratic outlook earned admiration during his 1920s goodwill world tours.

As King, Edward antagonized Tory Prime Minster Stanley Baldwin by outspokenly sympathizing with poorly paid workers and supposedly admiring Nazi Germany. Edward's liaison with married Mrs Simpson embarrassed the royal family and when her divorce came through Baldwin opposed his marriage plans. Edward abdicated and accepted the title Duke of Windsor (1936). In 1937 he married Mrs Simpson and then lived abroad, unreconciled with the the royal family. In World War II Edward was Governor of the Bahamas (1940-5). He died (of cancer) in Paris, but is buried near Windsor.

GEORGE VI 1936-1952
Authority King of United Kingdom of Great Britain and Northern Ireland and British dominions overseas; Emperor of India until 22 June 1947; Head of the Commonwealth from 1949
Dynasty House of Windsor
Parents George, Duke of York (later George V) and Princess Mary of Teck (later Queen Mary), their second son
Born York Cottage, Sandringham, Norfolk 14 Dec 1895
Succeeded to the throne 11 Dec 1936
Crowned Westminster Abbey 24 May 1937
Reigned 15 years, 57 days

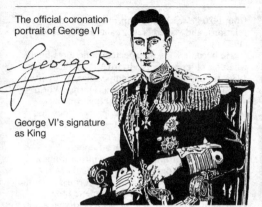

The official coronation portrait of George VI

George VI's signature as King

Died Sandringham House, Norfolk 6 Feb 1952
Buried St George's Chapel, Windsor Castle, Berks
Married Lady Elizabeth Bowes-Lyon (born 4 Aug 1900), youngest daughter of Claude Bowes-Lyon, 14th Earl of Strathmore and Kinghorne, 26 Apr 1923 at Westminster Abbey
Children Elizabeth (Elizabeth II) and Margaret (b1930)
Key facts George won national admiration for strong devotion to duty in war and for mastering a stammer threatening his public speaking commitments.

   Prince Albert, the future king, served in the Royal Navy in World War I, and attended Trinity College, Cambridge (1919-20). As Duke of York,

from 1920 he worked to improve industrial
relations, and visited New Zealand and Australia
(1927-8).

He became King unexpectedly and unwillingly
when his elder brother Edward VIII abdicated in
1936. In 1939 he became the first reigning British
monarch to visit North America. During World
War II he lived in London despite frequent
bombing raids, and visited troops in France and
North Africa. His Christmas broadcasts boosted
public morale.

After the war his reign saw a Labour
government transforming Britain into a welfare
state. In 1949 George VI became Head of the
Commonwealth of Nations, newly formed from the
fragmenting British Empire. He opened the
Festival of Britain in 1951 but died next year soon
after an operation for lung cancer.

ELIZABETH II 1952-
Authority Queen of the United Kingdom of Great
Britain and Northern Ireland and other realms and
territories; Head of the Commonwealth and Head
of State for 16 of its members
Dynasty House of Windsor
Parents Duke of York (later George VI) and
Duchess of York (later Queen Elizabeth, in
widowhood the Queen Mother)
Born 17 Bruton St, London W1 21 Apr 1926
Succeeded to throne 6 Feb 1952
Crowned Westminster Abbey 29 May 1953
Reigned 38 years to date

Elizabeth II's signature

The Queen's personal standard adopted in 1960 to symbolize her status as Head of the Commonwealth

Married Philip, Duke of Edinburgh (born 10 June 1921), only son of Prince Andrew of Greece and Princess Alice, great-grand daughter of Queen Victoria, 20 Nov 1947 at Westminster Abbey

Children Charles, Prince of Wales (born 14 Nov 1948), Anne, Princess Royal since 1987 (born 15 Aug 1950), Andrew, Duke of York (born 19 Feb 1960), Edward (born 10 Mar 1964)

Key facts Queen Elizabeth II has maintained the symbolic role of national figurehead played by all British monarchs since Edward VII.

She was educated privately, and during World War II trained in military motor transport with the Auxiliary Territorial Service. In 1947 she married

Above: Buckingham Palace, the Queen's principal residence

The oldest Crown Jewels, the Golden Eagle Ampulla, for the Holy Oil, and the Anointing Spoon

Lieutenant Philip Mountbatten of the Royal Navy, then newly created Duke of Edinburgh, and formerly Prince Philip of Greece.

Elizabeth became Queen early in 1952 while in Africa on a royal tour. Crowned in 1953, she made Philip a prince of the United Kingdom in 1957.

As Head of State, Head of the Commonwealth, and patron of various charities, she has kept up an arduous programme of official openings, inspections, and tours, including state visits to most corners of the Commonwealth and to non-Commonwealth countries.

Among the Queen's chief personal interests is the owning and running of racehorses.

Elizabeth II at her coronation, wearing St Edward's Crown, and holding the Royal Sceptre and Orb. All three Crown Jewels were made for Charles II's 1661 coronation

Monarchs, including their consorts from Egbert (802-839) onwards, and regional kingdoms are indexed below. The reader is urged to use the contents pages and top of the page headings to find English and Scottish dynasties such as the House of Windsor. Figures in **bold type** indicate an individual king's main entry. *Italics* denote an illustration reference. A monarch's appearance in a dynastic chart is indicated by the suffix 'd' after a page number.

Adela of Louvain 116d, 124
Adelaide, Queen 210-11d, 223
Aed Finnliath 78
Aedh 86d, 88
Aelfwald 24
Aelle 18-19
Aesc 16
Aescwine of Essex 20
Aescwine of Wessex 38
Aidan, King of Scots 31
Aileach, Kingdom of 78, *81*
Alba, Kingdom of 88, 89
Albert, Prince 225, 226, 229, 230d
Alchred 34
Aldfrith 33
Aldgyth, Queen 54
Aldwulf of E Anglia 24
Aldwulf of Sussex 20
Alexander I 92d, 95
Alexander II 92d, 97
Alexander III 92d, 97, 98, *98*
Alexandra of Denmark 230d, 231, *231*, 236
Alfred 40, **41-2**, *41*, 56, 57, 68
Allectus, Caius 10
Alric 18
Ambrosius Aurelianus 11
Anarawd 68
Androco 7
Anglo-Saxon kings 13-56
Anna 24, 37
Anne of Bohemia 149d, 151
Anne of Cleves 171d, 177
Anne of Denmark 190-1d, 193, 194

Anne of Great Britain 190d, **206-8**, *207*, *208*
Anne, the Princess Royal 234d, 247
Antoninus Pius, Emperor 9
Arthur (Artorius Rex) 11-12, 13
Arwald 19
Athelstan I of E Anglia 25
Athelstan of England, 43, **44-5**, 58, 89
Atrebates, Kings of the 6

Balliol, Edward 93d, 101, **103**
Balliol, John 93d, **99**, 144
Beaufort, Joan 104d, 108
Beohrtric 39
Beonred 28
Beorhtwulf 30
Beornwulf 29, 39
Berengaria of Navarre 130d, 135
Berhtun 19
Bernicia, Kingdom of 30, 31, 32, 35
Bethoc, Queen 87d, 90
Bleddyn ap Cynfyn 70
Boleyn, Anne, 171d, 177, 184
'Bonnie Prince Charlie' *see* Stuart, Charles Edward
Boudicca (Boadicea) 7, *7*
Bretwalda 15, 19, 22, 32, 33, 36
Brian Boru 79, 81
Brigantes, Kings and Queens of the 7
Bruce, Edward 101, *see also* Robert I
Burgred 30

Cadell 68
Cadwalla *see* Caedwalla
Cadwalla of Wessex 19, 38
Cadwallon ap Cadwan 67
Cadwallon ap Idwal 69
Caedwallada of Gwynedd 27, 32, **67**
Canute 44, 51, 52, 57, 59, **60-2**, *61*
Caradoc (Caractacus) 7
Carausius, Marcus Aurelius 10
Caroline of Ansbach 210d, 214, 216
Caroline of Brunswick 210-11d, 220, 221
Cartimandua 7
Caswallon 7
Cathal O'Connor 80
Catherine of Aragon 171d, 175, *176*, 177, 183
Catherine of Braganza 190d, 198
Catherine of Valois 154d, 156, 157d, 170
Catuvellauni, Kings of the 7
Ceawlin 36
Cenfus 38
Centwine 38
Cenwalh 37
Cenwulf 29
Ceol 37
Ceolred 28
Ceolwulf I 29
Ceolwulf II 30
Ceolwulf of Northumbria 33, 34
Ceolwulf of Wessex 37
Ceorl 26
Cerdic 36
Ceredig 67
Charles I 190-1d, 193, *193*, **194-7**, *195, 196, 197*, 198, 200
Charles II 190d, 196, **197-200**, *198, 199*
Charles, Prince of Wales 234d, 247
Charlotte, Queen 210d, 218, *218*, 220, 223
Cissa 19

Claudius I, Emperor 9
Clodius Albinus 9-10
Cnut, *see* Canute
Coel the Splendid, *see* Old Coel the Splendid
Coenred of Mercia 28
Coenred of Northumbria 33
Coenwulf 29
Cogidubnus (Cogidumnus) 8
Commius 6
Condidan 37
Conmail 37
Connaught, Kings and Kingdom of 77, *81*
Constans, Emperor 10
Constantine I of Scotland 86d, 88
Constantine II of Scotland 86d, 88
Constantine III of Scotland 86d, 89
Constantine the Great 10
Constantine III, usurper-Emperor 11
Constantius Chlorus I, Emperor 10
Cormac mac Art 77
Creoda 26
Cuilean 86d, 89
Cunedda 66-67
Cunobelinus 7
Cuthred 38
Cynan ap Hywel 69
Cynegils 37
Cynewulf 38, 39
Cynric 36

Dafydd ap Gruffydd 74
Dafydd ap Owain 71
Dalriada, Kings and Kingdom of 78, *81*, 82-3
David I 92d, **95**, *96*, 99
David II 93d, **101-2**, *102*
David ap Llywelyn 72, *73*
Deheubarth, Kings and Kingdom of 66-72
Deira, Kings and Kingdom of 30-32, 60

Dhubh 87d, 89
Donald I 86d, 88
Donald II 86d, 88
Donald III 87d, 90, 94
Donnchad 79
Drummond, Annabella 104d, 107
Dublin, Norse Kingdom of 57, 58, 62, 65, 78-79
Dumnocoveros 7
Duncan I 87d, 90
Duncan II 92d, 94
Dyfed, Kingdom of 68

Eadbald 17
Eadbert of Northumbria 34
Eadbert I 17
Eadbert II Praen 18
Eadric 17
Eadwig, *see* Edwy
Ealhswith, Saxon Queen 42
Eanfrith 32
Eanred 35
Earconbert 17
Eardwulf of Kent 18
Eardwulf of Northumbria 35
East Anglia, Kings of 22-25, 24
Ecgric 24
Edgar of England 45, **47-9**, *48*, 50, 89
Edgar of Scotland 92d, **94-5**
Edgar the Atheling 55, 94
Edith, Queen 52
Edgifu, Queen 43, 45
Edmund of E Anglia 25
Edmund I 43, **45-6**, 47, 58, 68
Edmund II 50, **51-2**, 62
Edred 43, **46**, 59
Edward I 74, 98, 99, 100, 130-1d, 140, **141-4**, *143*, 145
Edward II 74, 93d, 99, 101, 131d, 142, **144-6**, *144*, *146*
Edward III 65, 101, *102*, 103, 131d, *144*, 145, **146-50**, *148*, 149d, *150*, 152, 173, 219
Edward IV 160, 162-3d, **164-6**, *165*, 168

Edward V 163d, **166-7**, 170
Edward VI 171d, 178, **180-1**, *181*, 182, 184
Edward VII 225, **229-33**, 230d, *232*, *233*, 236, 247
Edward VIII 234d, 236, **241-4**, *242*, *243*, 246
Edward the Confessor **52-4**, *53*, 57, 90, 119, *151*
Edward the Elder 36, **42-3**, *43*, 44, 46, 88, 89
Edwin 23, 26, 27, **32**, 37, 67
Edwy 45, **47**
Egbert I of Bernicia 35
Egbert II of Bernicia 35
Egbert II of Kent 18
Egbert III, *see* Egbert of Wessex
Egbert of Wessex 18, 20, 22, 29, 30, **39-40**, *39*, 43-4
Egfrith of Mercia 29
Egfrith of Northumbria 27, **33**
Egwina 43, 44
Eleanor de Montfort 72
Eleanor of Aquitaine 130d, 132, 134, 137
Eleanor of Castile 130-1d, 142, *143*, 145
Eleanor of Provence 130d, 140, 141
Elizabeth I 113, 171d, 172, 181, **184-7**, *185*, 186, *187*
Elizabeth II 229, 234-5d, 245, **246-9**, *247*, *248*, *249*
Elizabeth de Burgh 93d, 101
Elizabeth of York 163d, 164, 171d, 173, 175, 176
Elizabeth, the Queen Mother 245, 246
Elizabeth Woodville 162d, 164, 166, 167, 170
Ella 35
Elmet, Kingdom of 32
Emma of Normandy 50, 60, *63*, 64
Eocha 86d, 88
Eochaid IV 85

Eormenric 16
Eorpwald 23, 24
Eppillus 6
Eric Bloodaxe 46, 58, **59**
Eric of E Anglia 57
Ermengarde de Beaumont 92d, 97
Essex, Kings of 20-22
Ethelbald of Mercia 22, **28**, *29*, 38
Ethelbald of Wessex 40
Ethelbert I **16**, 36
Ethelbert II 17
Ethelbert of E Anglia 25
Ethelbert of Wessex 41
Ethelfled, Queen 48, 49
Ethelfleda, Lady of the Mercians 43
Ethelfrith 31
Ethelheard 38
Ethelhere 24
Ethelred of Mercia 27
Ethelred I of Northumbria 34
Ethelred II of Northumbria 35
Ethelred I of Essex 41
Ethelred II of England **50-1**, 60
Ethelric of Bernicia 31
Ethelwald Moll 34
Ethelwalh 19
Ethelweard 25
Ethelwold 24
Ethelwulf 30, **40**
Euphemia Ross 104d, 107

Fergus of Dalriada 78, **82**, 85
Flann Sinna 76

Geoffrey IV of Anjou 124, 127, 128, 129, 132
George I **209-13**, *209*, 210d, *212*
George II 210d, **213-16**, *214*, *215*
George III 210d, **216-20**, 216, 217, 218, 225
George IV 80, 210-11d, 219, **220-2**, *221*, *222*, 225
George V 230d, 232, 234d, **236-41**, *236*, *237*, *238-9*, 241, 244

George VI 234d, 236, **244-6**, *245*
Giric I 86, 88d
Giric II 87d, 89
Godfred I Crovan 65
Gododdin, Kingdom of 12, 33
Grey, Lady Jane 171d, 172, 181, **182-3**, *182*
Gruach ('Lady Macbeth') 87d, 90
Gruffydd ap Cyan 69, **70**, 71
Gruffydd ap Llywelyn 69
Gruffydd ap Llywelyn the Great *73*
Gruffydd ap Rhys 70
Guthfrith of Dublin 58
Guthfrith of York 57
Guthrum 23, **57**
Gwynedd, Kings and Kingdom of 49, 64-74

Hadrian, Emperor 9
Halfdan Ragnarson 57
Hardecanute 53, 60, **64**, 65
Harold I 60, **62-3**
Harold II 53, **54-6**, *55*, 70, 119-20
Hengest 15, 16
Henrietta Maria **191-2**, 196, 198, 200
Henry I 70, 92d, 94, 95, *114*, 116d, 118, **122-5**, *123*, 126, 127, 129
Henry II 71, 80, 96, 97, 126, 127, **129-34**, 130d, *132*, *133*, 137, 138
Henry III 72, 92d, 97, 98, 138, **139-41**, *139*, *140*
Henry IV 74, **152-6**, *153*, 154d
Henry V 154d, 155, **156-9**, *157*, *158*
Henry VI 154d, 157, **159-61**, *161*, 164, 166, 168
Henry VII 75, 105d, 109, 167, 171, **172-4**, 173-5, 176
Henry VIII 75, 80, 110, 171d, 173, **175-80**, *176*, *177*, *179*, 180, 182, 183, 184

Heptarchy 13, 15
High Kings of Ireland 76-80
Hlothere 17
Horsa 15
Howard, Catherine 171d, 178
Hun Beonna 24
Hwicce, Kingdom of 26, 27, 37
Hywel ab Idwal 69
Hywel Dda 68, *75*

Iago ab Idwal I 68
Iago ab Idwal II 69
Icel 26
Iceni, King and Queen of the 7-8
Ida 31
Idwal Foel 68
Indulf 86d, 89
Ine 28, **38**
Ingibjorg, Queen 91, 92d, 94
Isabella de Warenne 92d, 99
Isabella of Angoulême 130d, 138, 139
Isabella of France (Edward II) 131d, *145, 145*, 146
Isabella of France (Richard II) 149d, 151
Isabella of Gloucester 130d, 138
Isabella of Mar 93d, 101
Isles, Lords of the 65, 109

James I of Great Britain *188*, **189-94**, *192, 193*, 209, 212
James I of Scotland 104d, **107-8**
James II of Great Britain 80, 190d, 196, **200-3**, *201, 202, 203*, 204, 205, 207
James II of Scotland 104d, **108**
James III of Scotland 104-5d, **108-9**
James IV of Scotland 105d, **109-10**, 171d, 175
James V of Scotland 105d, **110**, 190-1d
James VI of Scotland 105d, 113, *see* James I of Great Britain
James (VIII) the Old Pretender 190d, 202

Jane Seymour 171d, 177, 178, 180
Joan, Princess of Gwynedd 72
Joan, Queen of Scotland 92d, 97
Joan of Navarre 154d, 155
Joanna, Queen of Scotland 93d, 101, 103
John 72, 80, 92d, 97, 130d, 132, 134, *136*, **137-9**
Jorvik, *see* York
Judith, Saxon Queen 40

Kenneth I MacAlpin 82, **85**, 86d, **88**
Kenneth II 49, 87d, 89
Kenneth III 87d, 89, 90
Kent, Kings of 15-18
Leinster, Kings and Kingdom of 77, *81*
Lindsey, Kingdom of 27, 32, 33
Llywareh ap Hyfaidd 68
Llywelyn ap Gruffydd (Llwelyn the Last) *72*, 74
Llywelyn ap Iorweth (Llywelyn the Great) **71-2**, *73*, 75
Llywelyb ap Seisyll 69
Lords of the Isles 65, 109
Ludeca 30
Lulach 83, 85, 87d, 91

Macbeth 83, 85, 87d, **90**, 91
Maccus of Man 49
Macmurrough, Dermot 79-80
Madog ap Gruffydd 71
Madog ap Maredudd 70-1
Maelgwyn Hir 67
Mael Sechnail II
Magnus II of Man 65
Magnus Maximus, usurper-Emperor 10, 66
Malcolm I 46, 86-7d, **89**
Malcolm II 87d, **89-90**
Malcolm III 90, **91-4**, 92d, 98, 121, 124
Malcolm IV **95-6**, *96*, 97
Malcolm of Strathclyde 49, 84

Man, Isle and Kings of 65, 141, 146
Maredudd ap Edwin 69
Maredudd ap Owain 69
Margaret Drummond 93d, 103
Margaret, Maid of Norway 92d, **98-9**
Margaret of Anjou 154d, 160, 166
Margaret (Anjou) of Scotland 92d, 98
Margaret of France 130-1d, 142
Margaret (Tudor) of Scotland 109, 171d, 173, 175
Margaret, Saint 92d, 94
Mary I 171d, 181, **183-4**
Mary II 190d, 201, 202, 204, **205-6**, *206*
Mary, Queen of Scots 83, 105d, **110-12**, 112, 186, 189, 190-1d
Mary of Guelders 104d, 108
Mary of Guise 105d, 110, 190-1d
Mary of Modena 190d, 201, *203*
Mary of Teck (Queen Mary) 230d, 234d, 236, 241, 244
Matilda, Empress 95, 115, 116d, **126-8**, *127*, 129, 132
Matilda of Boulogne 116d, 125
Matilda of Flanders 116d, 118, 120, 122
Matilda of Scotland 116d, 124, 127
Meath, Kings of *76*, 77-78, 80, *81*
Mercia, Kings and Kingdom of 25-30, 42-3, 47, 48
Merfyn Frych 67
Munster, Kings and Kingdom of 77, 79, *81*
Mure, Elizabeth 104d, 107

Natanleod 36
Neville, Anne 162-3d, 168, *169*
Niall of the Nine Hostages 78
Northumbria, Kings of 30-35, 43, 47, 48
Nothelm 19
Nunna 19-20

O'Connor, Cathal 80
O'Connor, Rory 79-80
Octa 16
Offa of Essex 22
Offa of Mercia 20, **28**, 39
Olaf I **78**, 88
Olaf II 45, **58**
Olaf Sihtricsson 58
Old Coel the Splendid 12
Orkney, Earls of 65, 90, 91
Osbald 34
Osberht 35
Osmund 20
Osred I 33
Osred II 34
Osric 33
Oswald I 27, **32**, 67
Oswini 17
Oswulf 34
Oswy 32-33
Owain ap Hywel 68, 69
Owain Glyndwr (Owen Glendower) **71**, 156
Owain Gwynedd 71
Owain of Rheged 12
Owen, *see* Owain

Parr, Catherine 171d, 178
Peada 27, 33
Penda 24, **27**, 28, 32, 37, 67
Philip II of Spain 171d, *183*, 184
Philip, Duke of Edinburgh 234-5d, 247, 248
Philippa of Hainault 147, 149d
Picts, Kings of the 84-5
Powys, Kings and Kingdom of 66-74
Prasutagus 7
Pybba 26

Ragnald I 58
Ragnald II 58
Ranald of Dublin 78
Ranald of Waterford 79
Redburga, Queen 40
Redwald **23**, 32
Regni, Kings of the 8

Rheged, Kingdom of 12, 33
Rhodri Mawr **67**, 68
Rhys ap Gruffydd 71
Rhys ap Maredudd 74
Rhys ap Tewdwr 70
Richard I 97, 130d, 132, **134-7**, *135*
Richard II 80, 129, 149d, **151-2**, 155
Richard III 129, 162-3d, 167, **168-70**, *169*, 175
Robert I the Bruce 91, 93d, **99-100**, *100*, 103, 106, 144, 145
Robert II 79, 103, 104d, **106-7**, *106*
Robert III 104d, **107**
Roman rulers 9-12

Saelred 22
Seaxburgh, Queen 37
Sebbi 21
Septimius Severus, Emperor 9
Sibylla, Queen of Scotland 95
Sigeberht I 21
Sigeberht II 21
Sigeberht of E Anglia 23-4
Sigeberht of Wessex 38, 39
Sigered 22
Sigeric 22
Sigheard 22
Sighere 21
Sihtic Caoch of Dublin 58
Sledda 21
Somerled 65, 96
Stephen 95, *114*, 115, 116, **125-6**, *125*, 128
Strathclyde, Kings and Kingdom of 12, 34, 46, 49, 82, **83-4**, 88, 89
Stuart, Charles Edward, the Young Pretender 190d
Suaebhard 17
Swafred 22
Sweyn 44, 51, **59-60**
Swithhelm 21
Swithred 22

Tasciovanus 7
Tincommius 6
Togodumnus 7
Trahaiarn 70
Turgeis 78
Turlough More O'Connor 79
Tytila 23

Ulster, Kings and Kingdom of 77, 81, *81*
Urien 12

Verica 6
Victoria 209, 211d, **225-8**, *226*, 227, 228, 229, 230d, 232
Volisios 7
Vortigern 13, **15**

Wales, Kings and Princes of 66-75
Wiglaf 30
Wihtred 17
William I 53, 55-6, 57, 94, *114*, **115-20**, 116d, *118-19*, 122
William II 70, 94, *114*, 116d, **120-2**, *121*, 124
William III 80, 190d, 202, **203-5**, *204*, 206
William IV 210d, 219, **222-4**, *223*, *224*
William I of Scotland 92d, **96-7**
Woden 13, *14*, 20
Wuffa 22, 23
Wulfhere 19, **27**, 28
Yolande, Queen of Scotland 92d, 98
York, Norse Kings and Kingdom of 43, 56-9, 68, 78, *see also* Northumbria